BUILDING and CONNECTING Learning Communities

BUILDING and CONNECTING Learning Communities

The Power of Networks for School Improvement

Steven Katz

Lorna M. Earl

Sonia Ben Jaafar

CORWIN
A SAGE Company

For information:

Corwin
A SAGE Company
2455 Teller Road
Thousand Oaks, California 91320
(800) 233-9936
Fax: (800) 417-2466
www.corwinpress.com

SAGE India Pvt. Ltd.
B 1/I 1 Mohan Cooperative Industrial Area
Mathura Road, New Delhi 110 044
India

SAGE Ltd.
1 Oliver's Yard
55 City Road
London EC1Y 1SP
United Kingdom

SAGE Asia-Pacific Pte. Ltd.
33 Pekin Street #02-01
Far East Square
Singapore 048763

Printed in the United States of America

Library of Congress Cataloging-in-Publication Data

Katz, Steven, PhD.
Building and connecting learning communities : the power of networks for school improvement / Steven Katz, Lorna M. Earl, Sonia Ben Jaafar.
    p. cm.
Includes bibliographical references and index.
ISBN 978-1-4129-6600-9 (cloth)
ISBN 978-1-4129-6601-6 (pbk.)

    1. School management and organization. 2. Professional learning communities. 3. School improvement programs. 4. Educational leadership. I. Earl, Lorna M. (Lorna Maxine), 1948- II. Ben Jaafar, Sonia, 1974- III. Title.

LB2805.K368 2009
371.2'07—dc22   2009019905

This book is printed on acid-free paper.

09   10   11   12   13   10 9 8 7 6 5 4 3 2 1

Acquisitions Editor:	Debra Stollenwerk
Associate Editor:	Julie McNall
Production Editor:	Amy Schroller
Copy Editor:	Susan Jarvis
Typesetter:	C&M Digitals (P) Ltd.
Proofreader:	Gail Fay
Indexer:	Judy Hunt
Cover Designer:	Karine Hovsepian

Contents

Preface

THE RATIONALE

There seems to be an intuitive notion that "together is better," especially when it comes to professional learning. The concept of professional learning networks, with built-in ideas like commonality of purpose, reciprocity, exchange, and so on, seems to be a good fit for taking up the capacity-building challenges in education. Indeed, the educational landscape is well populated with professional learning communities (PLCs) of various sorts. The problem is that the pace of takeup of PLCs as a "good idea" far exceeds the evidence we have about their effectiveness. When we work with groups of educators—even very large ones—a favorite question of ours is to ask who is in a PLC. Without exception, a very healthy majority of hands go up. Where things get complicated is when we start to dig a little deeper and ask what being in a PLC actually means. What we find is that it means everything to everybody—voluntary "lunch and learns," after-school book studies, scheduled grade and division team encounters, focused lesson studies, and much, much more. And because being "in it together" makes such good intuitive sense, appealing to a basic need for affiliation as human beings, very few people push forward to ask the critical question, Does it translate into changed classroom practice and improved student learning and achievement?

What we find when we look at the research on professional learning collectives of various sorts is that together *can* be better—but it can also make no difference at all or even make things worse. It can preserve the status quo and make change more difficult. Our impetus for writing this book was to draw on our professional development and research experience to unpack the kinds of collaborative professional learning opportunities that can impact positively on student learning and achievement. You will see that these kinds of PLCs work by ratcheting up the quality of classroom practice in focused ways. They do so by building new understandings that are the foundations of impactful practice. And you will see that these kinds of learning communities are both established and strengthened by linking them with others. This book is about networked learning communities (NLCs)—within-school learning communities that are networked together in purposeful ways. Their mandate is one of professional knowledge creation and sharing for the purpose of enhancing the quality of classroom practice in a needs-based way.

OUR APPROACH

This book has emerged from our ongoing involvement in, and investigation of, a wide range of "NLCs" in education. Over multiple years, we have been engaged in an intensive "development and research program" in both North America and the United Kingdom. We have worked with multiple school districts and jurisdictions to implement NLCs as a central school improvement strategy. We say "development and research" because the relationship has been practice driven and iterative. We take our best shot, we learn from it in a systematic and research-based way, we refine practice on the basis of the evidence, we try again, and so on. In this book, we hope to share our learning and thinking about the challenging process of continuous professional learning in the complex world of schooling. We firmly believe that professional educators are key players in the move from twentieth-century schools with a mandate to teach the elite and sort the rest, to twenty-first-century schools with an obligation to prepare all students for the knowledge society in which they will live and work. We have not written a "how-to" book with lists of tips for teachers but we have tried to contextualize our learning in real situations that we have experienced, and provide examples and stories that can be used as a foundation for discussion among education professionals.

ORGANIZATION

The book is organized into eight chapters. In Chapter 1, we have situated networks as having considerable promise as a mechanism for building and sharing professional knowledge in ways that can have an influence on what teachers do in classrooms every day with students in the pursuit of more and better learning for all. Chapter 2 describes how NLCs work—both in theory and from research. The next three chapters give detailed accounts of the three key enablers of professional learning within networks. Chapter 3 explores the importance of having a clear, evidence-based focus and gives some suggestions about how to identify a defensible and high-leverage learning focus. Chapter 4 describes collaborative inquiry that challenges thinking and practice, as a process for new learning for teachers, in the service of new learning for students. Chapter 5 examines the role of leaders, both formal and informal, in both PLCs and NLCs. Chapter 6 is about how the key enablers work together to create the conditions for focused professional learning for teachers. Chapter 7 extends the professional learning requirement from learning for teachers to learning for leaders, and it considers the role of the network in creating the requisite conditions. In Chapter 8, we move to the issue of sustainability and continuity in NLCs.

READING AND USING THIS BOOK

This book will be of interest to teacher leaders, school administrators, and those—like superintendents—with responsibility for leading district-level change. Throughout the book, we have embedded a narrative drawn from our experiences working with numerous networks in different countries and contexts to give the reader a firsthand view of the intricacies and challenges associated with making NLCs work. Each of the professional roles noted above is reflected within it, and you will likely see yourself and your district represented. You can read the book with or without the narrative, depending on the degree to which you want to "see" what it looks like. The book can be read straight through, or it can be a resource for learning and conversation among school and district teams. In the service of the latter, we have ended each chapter with a reflection task for your group to use to think about how the information included in the prior chapter relates to you and your context.

Acknowledgments

This book is the product of an ongoing "development and research" agenda, and couldn't have been possible without a range of partners in the field who, like us, were and are committed to an iterative cycle of trying, learning, and refining. We are grateful to David Jackson, the former director of the Networked Learning Group at the National College of School Leadership in England, who brought us on board to evaluate what was likely the largest school-to-school networked learning initiative of its kind in the world. From the outset, David was clear that the evaluation needed to be conceptualized as formative, as a systematic way to learn about what worked and why so that the learning could be purposefully harnessed to inform successive sets of next steps. The knowledge with which we came away as the product of our work in England gave us an opportunity to share our learning and continue to refine the ideas.

We have been fortunate to partner with several school districts back on this side of the Atlantic who have been interested in, and committed to, continuing to learn with us. In particular, our partnership with the York Region District School Board has been especially invaluable. Superintendent of Schools Robert Dunn initiated, supported, and championed networked learning in York Region and has worked with us as we have continued to refine key ideas and practices over several years in an environment that has valued the transparency of learning in the focused pursuit of student achievement. And we have seen the results. Other superintendents in York Region and in Niagara District have found ways to bring us into the networks of schools that they support, and allowed us to be a part of them over multiple years as we worked to learn and build capacity together. This is what job-embedded learning really means and we thank all of them very much. Of course, we would be nowhere without the administrators, consultants, coordinators, and teachers who invited us to their meetings, and into their schools and classrooms. You know who you are, and we are most grateful to you.

Finally, to the team of talented researchers who have supported our learning about learning networks over the many projects we have undertaken, we wouldn't be very far along without you. Thank you all. We are particularly indebted to Lisa Dack for the active role she has taken on multiple occasions on both the research and professional development dimensions of the work, and for her careful reading and suggestions on earlier drafts of this book that have helped to make it better.

Corwin gratefully acknowledges the contributions of the following reviewers:

Helen Timperley
Professor of Education
University of Auckland
Auckland, New Zealand

Lynn A. Kaszynski, PhD
Elementary School Principal
Harrison Street Elementary
Sunbury, OH

Nicky Kemp
Principal
North Callaway R1
Williamsburg, MO

Steve Knobl
High School Principal
Pasco County Schools
Gulf High School
New Port Richey, FL

Patricia Long Tucker
Instructional Superintendent
District of Columbia Public Schools
Washington, DC

About the Authors

Steven Katz, PhD, is a director with the research and evaluation firm Aporia Consulting Ltd. and a permanent faculty member in Human Development and Applied Psychology at the Ontario Institute for Studies in Education (OISE) of the University of Toronto. He is an associate member of the School of Graduate Studies and is the coordinator of the Psychology of Learning and Development initial teacher education program component.

Dr. Katz has a doctorate in human development and applied psychology, with a specialization in applied cognitive science. His areas of expertise include cognition and learning, teacher education, networked learning communities, and the design of data-driven systems for organizational accountability, planning, and improvement. He has received the Governor General's medal for excellence in his field, and has been involved in research and evaluation, professional development, and consulting with a host of educational organizations around the world.

Lorna M. Earl, PhD, is a director of Aporia Consulting Ltd. and a retired Associate Professor from the Department of Theory and Policy Studies at the Ontario Institute for Studies in Education of the University of Toronto. She was the first Director of Assessment for the Ontario Education Quality and Accountability Office, and she has been a researcher and research director in school districts for over twenty years. Dr. Earl holds a doctorate in Epidemiology and Biostatistics, as well as degrees in education and psychology.

Throughout her career, Dr. Earl has concentrated her efforts on policy and program evaluations as a vehicle to enhance learning for pupils and for organizations. She has done extensive work in the areas of literacy and the middle years, but has concentrated her efforts on issues related to evaluation of large-scale reform and assessment (large-scale and classroom) in many venues around the world. She has worked extensively in schools and school boards, and has been involved in consultation, research, and staff development with teachers' organizations, ministries of education, school districts, and charitable foundations.

 **Sonia Ben Jaafar,** PhD, is a research associate at Aporia Consulting Ltd. She works internationally to support policy and program development and implementation through applied research and evaluation. Her areas of expertise include assessment, accountability, educational reform, policy and program development, and comparative studies.

Dr. Ben Jaafar graduated from the Ontario Institute for Studies in Education of the University of Toronto with a PhD in Theory and Policy Studies. She also holds an MA in Curriculum, Teaching and Learning, a BEd specialized in science education, and a BSc in Biochemistry.

1

Why Networks? Why Now?

In his thought-provoking book *The Wisdom of Crowds*, James Surowiecki (2004) outlines the case for why the many are smarter than the few. He cites, as an example, the global response to the Severe Acute Respiratory Syndrome (SARS) disease epidemic, a response that can be held out as model of efficiency and success. The discovery of the SARS virus—the new virus that caused the disease—was, as Surowiecki describes it, a remarkable feat. And, as with any remarkable feat, our immediate question is, Who did it? As it turns out, that's an impossible question to answer. Why? Because it took a combined effort from labs all over the world to (a) spot the virus, (b) prove that the identified virus made people sick, and (c) differentiate it from a range of other possible viral candidates that had to be ruled out as the cause of the disease. Ultimately, no single person discovered the cause of SARS. The World Health Organization (WHO) attributes the discovery of the virus to a group of labs working collectively. Any one of those labs working on its own might have taken months or years to identify the virus but together they did in just a few weeks. What makes the collaboration especially noteworthy is that no one was officially in charge of it. Although the World Health Organization (WHO) orchestrated the creation of the network of labs, there was no central dictate telling each lab what to do. As Surowiecki (2004, p. 161) describes it:

> The collaborative nature of the project gave each lab the freedom to focus on what it believed to be the most promising lines of

investigation, and to play to its particular analytical strengths, while also allowing the labs to reap the benefits—in real time—of each other's data and analyses. And the result was that this cobbled-together multinational alliance found an answer to its problem as quickly and efficiently as any top-down organization could have.

The *Wisdom of Crowds*—and the case of SARS specifically—points to the promise and potential of collaborative mechanisms, like networks, for taking up problems of practice, whether in health or in education. Of course, it's not as simple as "together is always better." As we will show later, there are some very important preconditions that need to be in place. But under the right conditions (and this book is devoted to unpacking and understanding what those are), the many can indeed be smarter than the few and networks can be powerful organizational forms for school improvement.

> The world is becoming a networked environment. This is having a profound impact on the way we organize at the local, national and international level (Church et al., 2002, p. 1).

For decades, numerous school improvement models have attempted to reform the thinking and practices of practitioners with the explicit intent of increasing student success in schools. Introducing reforms into classrooms and schools generally has accomplished superficial changes to practices and outcomes that have not translated easily into sustainable improvement for student learning (D. Hargreaves, 2003). Professional networks increasingly are being promoted as mechanisms to intentionally create the level of deep learning necessary for practitioners that can lever the kinds of changes that make a difference for students.

IT'S ABOUT LEARNING

The Organization for Economic Cooperation and Development (OECD) study on sustainable flexibility (OECD, 1997) points to the changing nature of work and life in the knowledge society of the twenty-first century. In this society, lifelong learning is a cornerstone of the flexibility necessary for highly skilled and educated citizens to take on new tasks and continuously adapt to new and changing environments. As we exit the industrial age, characterized by a "finite" conception of resources, a "controllable" conception of information, and a "sequential and task-specific" conception of learning, the notion of networks takes on increased relevance (Allen & Cherrey, 2000). Specifically, networks provide an operational construct for educational provision and a new vehicle for achieving change.

In this knowledge society, practices for facilitating knowledge creation and sharing are considered to be the key tenets of educational provision. Knowledge will be, and perhaps already is, the most critical resource for social and economic development (Hakkarainen, Palonen, Paavola, & Lehtinen, 2004). Change-directed improvement comes from creating new knowledge or adding value to existing knowledge rather than simply appropriating existing knowledge resources. A fundamental challenge for education, then, is to organize work with knowledge in a way that facilitates ongoing knowledge building and sharing among members of the community. As Hakkarainen et al. (2004) remind us, members of the community need to develop competencies that allow them to function as "knowledge workers."

In *Working Laterally*, David Hargreaves (2003) describes the demands of knowledge creation (and the associated competencies that support it) in terms of innovation. Knowledge creation (or transformation) is, in a word, innovation. Young people need to be innovative to succeed in work and life, and education can both model this requirement and support its development. For teachers, innovation is about learning to work differently in order to work better. Most innovation is the creation of new professional knowledge about their work.

NETWORKS: A POWERFUL ORGANIZATIONAL TOOL

The question of how networks "work" in the service of the kind of educational reform that Hargreaves (2003) describes is one that for a long time was best answered in the tentative terms of "promise." The route is undoubtedly complex. Judith Chapman and David Aspin (2003) suggest the following possible pathways of function:

- Networks can offer a means of assisting in the policy implementation process by linking policy both horizontally and vertically.
- Networks can provide a process for cultural and attitudinal change, embedding reform in the interactions, actions, and behavior of a range of stakeholders.
- Networks can provide an opportunity for shared and dispersed leadership and responsibility, drawing on resources in the community beyond education.
- Networks can be capacity building insofar as they are able to produce new knowledge and mutual learnings that can feed back to and inform public policy.
- Networks can move attention away from a preoccupation with micro-level change at the individual site and function at the meso level to strengthen interconnections and spread innovation across all levels—micro, meso, and macro.

The educational landscape is populated by networks of many forms. In the United Kingdom, government-sponsored networks have developed to encourage and support continuous cooperative learning at all levels of the education system. In North America, the growth of organic networks of teachers and administrators has taken place over the past twenty years without a formal government-sponsored infrastructure. Some networks join teachers and/or schools together at the national, state, or provincial level. The National Writing Project, for example, is a teachers' national network of writing (Lieberman & Wood, 2002). In British Columbia, Canada, the Network of Performance Based Schools (NPBS) links schools with an "Assessment for Learning" focus (Katz, Earl, Ben Jafaar, 2008). Other networks are bound by jurisdiction, such as the Consortium for Educational Change, a network of school districts in Illinois created to improve student achievement by assisting member districts and schools to become collaborative, high-performing organizations. Likewise, the Bay Area School Reform Collaborative (BASRC) is a network of schools in the San Francisco Bay Area that collaborate to achieve equity-minded school reform (Center for Research on the Context of Teaching, 2003). The York Region District School Board in Ontario, Canada, has organized approximately twenty-two networks of elementary schools, each with a shared focus and geography.

Despite the considerable theoretical and intuitive promise of networks, and their increasing prevalence and popularity as an organizational form, there is little systematic research about the way networks work in educational contexts or about what to emphasize to foster successful and productive networked learning in education. Over the past few years, we have been engaged in a development and research agenda that has worked to fill this gap. We began in England, a forerunner in considering networks as an integral part of their policy landscape in education. In 2002, the National College of School Leadership established a four-year development and research initiative to support the implementation of networked learning communities (NLCs) in English schools and to learn from their experiences. We engaged in a large evaluation study of the Networked Learning Communities Program. NLCs were conceived as groups of school working together to enhance the quality of professional learning and to strengthen capacity for continuous improvement. The initiative was the largest of its kind in the world and comprised 132 networks that encompassed 1,500 schools, 43,000 teachers, and 690,000 students.

Our goal in this evaluation was not an outcome evaluation (i.e., did the program work or not?), but rather a forward-looking learning opportunity with a view to informing the field about the key features of NLCs and how these features work in practice. The study was timely given the proliferation of learning networks of various sorts around the world. What was particularly important was that we had the kind of data that allowed us to connect the features we identified to teacher practice and to student achievement—both critical outcomes for any school improvement methodology.

Armed with our empirically validated learning about the high-leverage practices of networks that make a difference for teachers and students, we became intentional about building and supporting learning networks of schools. We pushed forward with a development and research program in several school districts, taking our learning, translating it into practice, and then engaging in research designed to learn and feed forward into the next iteration of this work. The results of these efforts (which still continue to unfold) form the substance of this book.

As we noted in the Preface, an authentic narrative for exemplification of ideas and structured reflection opportunities run throughout the book. Below is the first installment of each.

Educational leaders face real-time issues in schools. Their ability to recognize an authentic need for improvement is an important start to responding appropriately.

Joan is the principal of Selkirk Elementary School, which has 634 students. According to the large-scale assessment results, the school is average. Selkirk has close to average numeracy results: the percentage of students reaching the standard in Selkirk is 2 percent greater than the state average and 4 percent greater than the district average. The literacy results are also close to average: the percentage of students reaching the standard in the school is 3 percent below state average and 7 percent below the district average. Most of the students attending the school are from families that are established in the community. About 10 percent of the families at the school have arrived in the country in the last five years. Most of the parents work in the trades or in professional jobs. There is a positive school culture, with most teachers choosing to stay in the school—the newest teachers in the school arrived at the same time as Joan, three years ago.

When Joan received the school's large-scale assessment results, a cursory look showed that the scores had not improved from last year. She was especially disappointed in the literacy results from the primary division because not only were they still just below the district average, but they had not improved at all in the last three years despite her school's improvement efforts.

Time for Reflection

Think of a professional situation when you worked in a group where the outcome was beneficial and another situation where it was unproductive. What do you think was the difference between the two situations that contributed to the success or failure of the collaboration?

2

How Networked Learning Communities Work

WHAT ARE NETWORKED LEARNING COMMUNITIES?

The concept of networks is a pretty broad and all-encompassing one. Search the Internet and you'll find networks used to describe everything that includes a dimension of interconnectivity—computers, telephones, and of course people. Most leaders, regardless of their field, will tell you that effective collaboration is essential to an organization's success. And they will tell you that they strive to create opportunities for collaboration. However, as Cross and Parker (2004) explain, such efforts—though expensive in resource terms—often yield few or no results. Why? Because bringing people together does not necessarily produce better outcomes, unless the collaborative work is organized to engage people in the process and is supported to move them beyond their established patterns. Cross and Parker (2004) cite popular organizational examples of managers implementing collaborative technologies with the vague notion that they will help employees interact more seamlessly and that this will automatically enhance the quality of their work, only to find that this kind of contrived collaboration (A. Hargreaves, 1994) has done little beyond being experienced as an impediment to the work! For networks to be effective, they need to do more than create connections.

At the beginning of Chapter 1, we looked at the power and potential of collective wisdom as illustrated in the case of SARS. In that example, together was clearly better than alone. But we can also point to other cases—as Surowiecki (2004) himself does—where together is in fact worse. The explosion of the space shuttle Columbia is one such example. A retrospective study of the disaster points to warning signs that were repeatedly missed because of the perils of collective wisdom. The field of social psychology has warned us of such dangers for decades through concepts like diffusion of responsibility, social loafing, group-think, and deindividuation. Diffusion of responsibility and social loafing are psychological phenomena that explain why people are *less* likely to take responsibility when they are in the presence of others (real or imagined) than when they are alone. Essentially, people are less likely to assume responsibility if they believe that someone else might do so. The end result is that nobody does anything because everyone thinks that someone else will! Group-think and deindividuation refer to the stifling of individuality and divergence within a collective context. For example, if you put a group of people in a room together and allow for a free-flowing discussion, the group will settle on content for which there is already high agreement among group members; sameness will trump diversity. And beyond these psychologically grounded dangers of the collective, we also have to worry about quality control. That is, when left to their own devices, networks will spread anything—and not necessarily what is worthy of sharing.

So what differentiates networks in which the many are smarter than the few from their less effective—or, worse, potentially damaging—counterparts? Surowiecki (2004) outlines four general parameters that, taken together, counteract the perils described above: diversity of opinion, independence, decentralization, and aggregation. "Diversity of opinion" means understanding that what makes strong groups is that they inject a degree of variability into the mix such that the range of options on which they might draw for decision making, problem solving, or capacity building is increased. "Independence" underscores the notion that a range of options will only exist if pressure for conformity is relaxed and everyone is free and comfortable to express different and/or unpopular opinions. The concept of "decentralization" recognizes that diversity and independence are bottom-up principles. They don't arise from top-down prescription but rather from localized, needs-based attempts to define and solve problems like, as we will see later, problems of practice. Finally, diversity of opinion, independence, and decentralization will only pay dividends at the group level if there is a mechanism for "aggregation," a way of bringing it all together so that there is benefit for the collective.

While the concept of networks is broad, there are some important general underpinnings or ideas that we will address in multiple ways and in multiple places as we work through the notion of one specific type of network: a networked learning community (NLC). This book isn't about networks in general. We are not concerned with electronic networks or with informal social networks, for example. We are focusing on the concept of a NLCs as articulated in the previous chapter in relation to the Networked Learning Communities Program in England. That is, we are interested in groups of schools working together in intentional ways to enhance the quality of professional learning and to strengthen capacity for continuous improvement, in the service of enhanced student learning. In the next section, we unpack this concept in more detail and frame the notion of an NLC as a network of within-school professional learning communities.

HOW NLCs WORK:
THE THEORY OF ACTION

Educators often ask the question, "Does it work in practice?" It's a good question, but it really isn't the first question that should be asked. Instead, the pertinent question is, "Does it work in theory?" If the hope is that it works in practice, it had better work in theory. Our initial network theory of action is illustrated in Figure 2.1. We built it, and then we tested it empirically and refined it. We began with a theory of action for NLCs based on an extensive review of the research literature. Very simply, the initial theory of action says that there is a logical relationship between what happens in NLCs and their ultimate goal of enhanced learning for students. The theory is that significant *changes in student learning* depend on major *changes in the practices and the structures of schools*, and these changes will emerge from the *professional knowledge creation and sharing* that occurs through interaction within and across schools in networks. This orientation to networks suggests that the influence of networked learning is based on knowledge creation theory—that learning and the creation of new knowledge by teachers and principals leads to deep conceptual changes and new ways of working in schools and classrooms. The key features of schools and networks that emerged from the research literature, and on which we elaborate below, are enablers that have the potential to create the conditions for this knowledge creation and sharing to occur in ways sufficiently powerful to result in significant changes in practice.

Figure 2.1 Key Features of NLCs

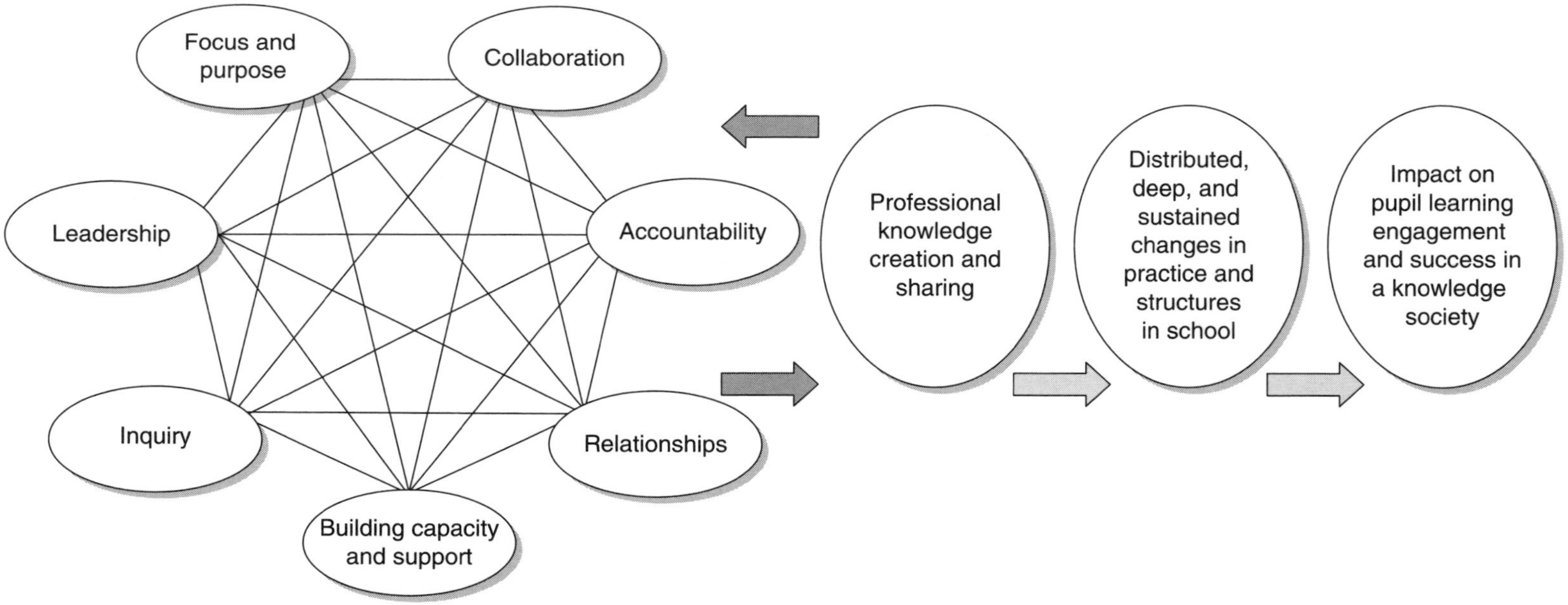

Source: Earl & Katz (2005).

According to this theory of action, NLCs are fundamentally about learning—learning for students, as well as learning for teachers, and learning for leaders. This is what distinguishes NLCs from other networks. Networks can exist for many reasons; in NLCs, the emphasis is on *learning*.

Historically, the route to understanding (and supporting) learning has focused on what individuals do "in their heads." More recently, learning theory has added the notion that knowledge creation is a process of participation in various cultural practices and shared learning activities, as well as a process of individual knowledge formation. Knowledge is created through dialogue or conversations that make presuppositions, ideas, beliefs, and feelings explicit and available for exploration. It is in these conversations that new ideas, tools, and practices are created, and the initial knowledge is either substantially enriched or transformed during the process (Hakkarainen et al., 2004). Innovative solutions arise when people in NLCs draw on outside explicit knowledge and combine it with tacit knowledge in response to authentic problems (Nonaka & Takeuchi, 1995; Von Krogh, Ichijo, & Nonaka, 2000). This theory of action suggests that NLCs work by creating the conditions for teachers, principals, and others in schools to move outside their typical contexts to engage with a broader scope of ideas and possibilities, and to participate in the kinds of professional conversations that create new knowledge and clarity that extends beyond what any one person entered with. Once new knowledge is created and shared, the expectation is that the new learning will *influence practices*. But simply changing structures is not enough to change (improve) practice (Elmore, 2002; Wohlstetter & Smith, 2000). Our theory of action suggests that the ultimate point of action is the school, where the conversations from the network stimulate the same kinds of conversations among teachers in the schools, encouraging them to challenge their thinking, share the new knowledge and internalize it, and moving them to make real changes in their thoughts and practices.

Engaging in NLCs is intended to foster the development of such professional learning communities (PLCs) in schools by linking school-based groups to their counterparts in other schools and by creating the conditions for knowledge creation and sharing. Several studies have found positive associations between the presence of PLCs within particular schools and the schools' success in enhancing student engagement and achievement (Bryk & Schneider, 2002; McLaughlin & Talbert, 2001). When the strength of attachment between schools and networks is strong, school-level learning communities can *upload* their ideas and practices into the network—thus strengthening the NLC. In the same way, school learning communities can *download* and use ideas and practices from the network for local knowledge creation and sharing. Individuals are the connectors

of schools to networks (and networks to schools), through active participation and through the construction of artifacts that serve as the link
between the network and the school, with a two-way flow.

In our initial theory of action, we proposed seven key enablers of successful NLCs, each of which operates within the schools and the network:
*(1) purpose and focus, (2) relationships, (3) collaboration, (4) inquiry, (5) leader-
ship, (6) accountability,* and *(7) capacity building and support.* Below, we provide a brief initial orientation to each of the enablers, and we unpack them
in more detail throughout the book. The key enablers are as follows:

Purpose and Focus

Having a fundamental and clear organizational purpose is critical to
the success of PLCs and NLCs. A learning focus is likely to have a more
direct impact if it is focused in ways that are concrete and useful
(Timperley & Robinson, 2003); high leverage in fostering student learning
(Marzano, Pickering, & Pollock, 2001); compelling, challenging, and
shared (Bryk, Camburn, & Louis, 1999; Lieberman & Grolnick, 1996); and
appropriate to the context (Marzano et al., 2001). A compelling and high-
leverage learning focus is based on evidence that it can have a significant
impact on teaching practices and student learning. A challenging focus is
one that requires teachers to reconceptualize, unlearn, or make changes to
existing practice and structures, legitimating the change process by making the status quo more difficult to protect, and offering opportunities for
joint attention to issues that are larger than any one school could address
alone (Timperley, 2004). Finally, the learning focus should be "right" for
the participating schools, given their particular context, history, and needs.

Relationships

Relationships are the "connective tissue" of NLCs (Allen & Cherry,
2000) and provide the social capital that allows people to work together
over time and exceed what any of them could accomplish alone (West-
Burnham & Otero, 2004). Relationships create a common language and a
sense of shared responsibility, provide channels for communicating and
disseminating information to one another about network members'
expertise, and develop readiness to trust one another (West-Burnham &
Otero, 2004).

Trust is a key condition of productive relationships. Indeed, Bryk and
colleagues (1999) found that social trust among members of staff was by
far the strongest facilitator of professional community. They propose that
a base level of such trust may be necessary for a professional community
to emerge, but working and reflecting together can also build trust and
strengthen relationships. In relationships, conflict is inevitable—and, as

we will see, valuable—but robust and trusting relationships amongst network members can allow them to work together even when they have different orientations and views (Lieberman & Grolnick, 1996).

Collaboration

Collaboration encompasses much more than relationships. It is intensive interaction that engages educators in opening up their beliefs and practices to investigation and debate. When colleagues engage in a dynamic process of interpretation and evaluation of practice, they enhance their own practice and that of the profession. This kind of collaboration allows people to address tough problems of teaching (Firestone & Pennell, 1997), build commitment through group understanding (Lieberman & Grolnick, 1996), solve issues of mutual concern (Wohlstetter & Smith, 2000), and spread innovations beyond individuals and single sites (Smith & Wohlstetter, 2001).

Collaboration can be a powerful mechanism for changing ideas and practices, particularly when it involves joint work that includes a balance of personal support with critical inquiry about present practice and future direction (Borko, 2004; Hudson-Ross, 2001) and sustained scrutiny of practice, but it is not always easy. In fact, moderate conflict is essential for the development of high joint benefit, and the desire to avoid conflict can undermine this outcome (Engestrom, 1999).

Inquiry

Systematic analysis of the situation and professional reflection are regarded as core activities for both individual and collective construction of meaning. We have written elsewhere about developing an inquiry habit of mind—a habit of using inquiry and reflection to think about where you are, where you are going, and how you will get there; and then turning around and rethinking the whole process to see how well it is working and making adjustments (Earl & Katz, 2006).

Knowledge creation—especially when people are involved in changing their practice—requires that individuals consider explicit knowledge and share, question, and possibly adapt their respective tacit knowledge in order to create new collective explicit knowledge. Little (2005) references a large body of research suggesting that conditions for improving learning and teaching are strengthened when teachers collectively question ineffective teaching routines, examine new conceptions of teaching and learning, find generative means to acknowledge and respond to difference and conflict, and engage actively in supporting one another's professional growth. The inquiry processes of questioning, reflecting, seeking alternatives, and weighing consequences promote the "transparency" of what otherwise might remain unobservable facets of practice, making tacit knowledge visible and open to scrutiny.

Collaborative inquiry creates an opportunity for educators to work together, searching for and considering various sources of knowledge (both explicit and tacit) in order to investigate practices and ideas through a number of lenses, putting forward hypotheses, challenging beliefs, and posing more questions. When educators have an inquiry habit of mind, they have developed a way of thinking that is a dynamic iterative system for organizing ideas, seeking out information, and moving closer and closer to understanding some phenomenon together.

Leadership

NLCs include many levels of leadership—both formal and informal. Although the leadership literature continues to emphasize the role of principals in successful change and instructional improvement, leadership models are increasingly focusing on what Rowan (1990) calls "network" patterns of control, where leadership activities are distributed across multiple people (Heller & Firestone, 1995). Formal leaders (e.g., principals) provide leadership by encouraging and motivating others, setting and monitoring the agenda, sharing leadership, providing support, and building capacity. At the same time, NLCs encourage distributed leadership in schools and across the network, with many people with and without formal positions of authority providing a range of leadership functions such as leading particular initiatives, participating in collaborative groups, supporting colleagues' learning, and sharing their knowledge with others.

Accountability

Accountability is the watchword of education, with policy makers demanding that schools focus on achieving high standards for all students, and requiring evidence of their progress. Both external and internal accountability have a role to play in how change happens.

External accountability in NLCs means being open and transparent in showing policy makers and the public what they are doing and how well it is working. Strong external accountability systems can also contribute to the achievement of a widely shared sense of purpose, create a sense of urgency, provide "pressure" for change, and offer a forum for conversation about the work of schools.

Internal accountability is a process of using evidence to identify priorities for change, to evaluate the impact of the decisions, to understand students' academic standing, to establish improvement plans, and to monitor and assure progress (Herman & Gibbons, 2001). As Elmore (2002) explains, the central problem of school improvement is knowing the right thing to do. To hold schools accountable for their performance depends on there being people in schools with the knowledge, skill, and judgment to make the improvements that will increase student performance.

Internal accountability is what moves the agenda from schools where teachers and leaders are working hard and showing enthusiasm for change to schools that are constantly engaged in careful analysis of their beliefs and their practices, to help them do things that they don't yet know how to do. This latter characterization is what lies at the heart of a professional *learning* community. And, as we will discuss shortly, networks "work" by transforming within-school PLCs.

Building Capacity and Support

Harris (2001) defines capacity building as being concerned with creating the conditions, opportunities, and experiences for collaboration and mutual learning. Years of school improvement research has shown that improving schools are ones that take charge of change, rather than being controlled by it (Stoll & Fink, 1996). As Senge (1990) describes it, a learning organization is one that is continually expanding its capacity to create its future. In NLCs, the focus is on creating the conditions to support individual and collective learning through all of the processes described in the previous key enablers. Building capacity depends on intentionally fostering and developing the opportunities for members to examine their existing beliefs and challenge what they do against new ideas, new knowledge, new skills, and even new dispositions. When networks are focused on learning, they intentionally seek out and/or create activities, people, and opportunities to push them beyond the status quo.

USING NLCS TO FOCUS LOCAL PLCS

This theory of action is founded on the strength of the processes and practices of successful PLCs in schools spreading beyond single sites to strengthen whole systems. A fair amount of work has been done on PLCs, most of it concerned with explicating the characteristics of what are deemed to be successful or effective PLCs. Particularly prominent within this body of literature is the work of DuFour and Eaker (1998), which identifies six characteristics of successful PLCs. These are (1) shared mission, vision, and values; (2) collective inquiry into questioning the status quo, seeking and testing new methods and reflectingon results; (3) collaboration; (4) an action and experimentation orientation; (5) an emphasis on continuous improvement; and (6) a results orientation.

Other researchers have highlighted quite similar characteristics. In their extensive literature review on PLCs, Bolam and colleagues (2005) identified five characteristics of effective PLCs: (1) shared values and vision; (2) collective responsibility for students' learning; (3) collaboration focused on learning; (4) individual and collective professional learning; and (5) reflective professional inquiry. To this list, the researchers added three additional characteristics that emerged from their own work: (1) openness and partnership; (2) inclusive membership; and (3) mutual trust, respect, and support. They define an effective PLC as one that has the capacity to promote and sustain the learning of all professionals in the school community with the collective purpose of enhancing student learning.

Despite a reasonable amount of consensus around what constitutes an effective PLC, real-world implementation has proved to be a much more difficult task. While it has been (relatively) easy to develop a myriad of structures that allow groups of educators to meet, a true focus on issues of practice has been a much more difficult challenge. Bolam et al. (2005) argue that a PLC's effectiveness should be judged on three criteria: (1) its ultimate impact on student learning and development; (2) its intermediate impact on professional learning, performance and morale; and (3) its operational performance. In their study of close to 400 within-school PLCs, they found sustainability on these three criteria to be relatively weak. In particular, they found that neither the impact of professional learning nor the process of PLC operation was normally monitored or evaluated, so there was no follow-up action to maximize their effectiveness.

Other researchers have concluded that, by and large, the majority of initiatives that self-identify as PLCs are not focused enough to guide teacher communities through the challenging task of critically exploring the relationship between what and how they teach, and student learning (Supovitz & Christman, 2005). In his in-depth investigation of the achievements of district-wide school improvement in Duval County, Florida, Jon Supovitz (2006) shows just how vast the gap between PLC theory and practice can be, even in a high-achieving context. When he asked school practitioners what it meant to be part of a PLC, he got a diversity of responses, of which the following are just a sample (pp. 174–176):

- "We read and share professional articles and books in our team meetings."
- "A community of learners, especially in this school, means that we speak the same language."
- "A community of learners is, first of all, empowering people to have a sense of parity within the system where they will have equal input into that process."
- "Continuous, continuous, continuous contact, continuous involvement, continuous dialogue, continuous problem-solving, continuous identifying strengths and weaknesses. It is continuity of effort."
- "Teachers get a chance to share ideas through their work—best practices, instructional practices."

Supovitz explains that while the concept of a PLC had clearly entered the district's lexicon and expanded interest in professional learning across the system, poor understanding of the concept led to generally thin enactment. As we ourselves have experienced in the multiple contexts of schooling in which we work, his findings confirm that rigorous inquiry into challenges of instructional practice and the support of that practice occur only in select pockets, if indeed at all. He concludes as follows (p. 178):

> The power of the idea of a professional learning community is that members of the group . . . engage together in challenges of practice so that their understanding of those challenges grows deeper and is more unified. Through their investigations, proposed solutions emerge that are then tested to see if they help. . . . Through such a repeated process, practice grows more sophisticated and powerful and the group develops a tighter sense of camaraderie and common purpose. As a result, they can construct common understanding, share knowledge and experience, and develop common goals. This form of professional learning communities was largely absent from the district, and the examples Duval County faculty members did provide were too diffused and unfocused to have a strong influence on their practice. Activities like book talks and in-school professional development sessions were too sparse and diffused to fulfill the particular goals promised by PLCs.

At this point, the urgent question becomes one of how school-level PLCs can ratchet up their work so that they can begin to deliver on their theoretical promise. Our take is that a promising catalyst comes by way of intentionally building networks of schools or, to put it more accurately, cross-school networks of within-school PLCs.

In a network of schools, the strengths of some schools' internal learning cultures can be a source of learning for other schools through network membership and activity. Networks of schools can both *build from* and *contribute to* within-school PLCs by providing the forum for established and positive organizational learning practices that are situated within school learning communities to be *uploaded* into the network and, in turn, *downloaded* to other sites.

Since Joan arrived at the school, she has worked hard to create a whole-school PLC focused on literacy.

PLCs had been a district-wide initiative for several years and, like others, Selkirk Elementary tried to create opportunities for groups of teachers to form such a community. Joan knew from previous training that successful PLCs needed to have a single mission that reflected the needs of the school. When she first arrived at the school and reviewed the school report card, she decided that literacy would be Selkirk's focus. Joan coordinated with her teachers so that, once a month, a staff meeting was dedicated to discussions about literacy. She scheduled teacher preparation time so that teachers teaching the same grade met together once every two weeks for forty minutes. Finally, she led a bimonthly lunch time book study group where staff could choose to eat their lunch while discussing their impressions of a reading about different literacy strategies. Joan discussed her efforts to promote a PLC in her school with other school leaders and she felt that she was making more efforts than many of her colleagues. However, notwithstanding the work of the PLC, nothing had changed in the school's assessment results and Joan was frustrated.

Joan came to the realization that her school PLC needed something more for greater success—so she sought out external insight. After her last book group meeting, Joan called Carl, her district administrator, and explained that she had been trying to understand why there had been no noticeable improvement in the Grade 3 literacy results for her school. She wanted to find out what the other schools were doing about literacy and asked whether she could raise the issue at the next family of schools administrator meeting. Carl agreed to have a discussion on the large-scale assessment results in the upcoming area meeting.

While the network does provide a mechanism for the transfer of knowledge between schools, it is not simply the broker of a parasite–host relationship where schools take from a network. Rather, a network has the potential to be generative, to be the source of knowledge creation. What this means is that, in addition to creating the possibility for within-school learning communities to learn *from* one another, the network can create opportunities for schools to learn *with* one another; to co-construct new knowledge. This is what we explored in Chapter 1 in connection with the wisdom crowds, where the outcome of working in a network is the creation of a whole that is greater than the sum of its parts. Thus, the relationship between network and school is a bidirectional, recursive one. NLCs allow schools to move beyond their own boundaries, a practice that is essential for innovation and advancement, even for the most highly functioning PLCs, and to learn together to go beyond what any of them might achieve on their own.

Our theory of action suggests that NLCs do their work by strengthening within-school PLCs in ways that allow them to become engines of professional learning that contribute to improved classroom practice. Moving to networked school-based PLCs requires much more than making connections and hoping that new learning will emerge by chance and transfer by osmosis. In the remainder of the book, we address the core enablers of NLCs that need to be intentionally developed, fostered, and nurtured to reap the benefits of working together: a clear and defensible network learning focus, collaborative inquiry that challenges thinking and practice, and formal and informal instructional leadership.

THE ANATOMY OF AN NLC: A REFINED THEORY OF ACTION

The key enablers of professional knowledge creation and sharing are the building blocks of effective learning communities, both within and across schools. They are dimensions of improvement that groups seek to intentionally create and support as the antecedents of professional learning that will change practice and influence student learning and achievement. In our continuing development and research agenda, we are coming to understand how the key enablers that we identified from the research literature (depicted in Figure 2.1) work as a constellation of enablers in schools and networks.

Key Enablers: Focus, Collaborative Inquiry, and Leadership

Figure 2.2 shows our refined thinking about the relationship of the within-school and between-school (network) learning communities, based on the evaluation of the Networked Learning Communities Program. It highlights three clusters of enablers, or rather enabling practices: the practice of establishing and supporting clear and defensible learning foci for students, teachers, and leaders; the practice of collaborative inquiry that challenges thinking and practice; and the practice of instructional leadership (both formal and informal). The "black" arrows (both the solid and the broken ones) represent the relationship between these enablers and both the school and the network. The solid arrows link the school and the enablers. The broken arrows link the network and the enablers. The message we are conveying is that, while the network does its work in terms of these enabling practices, it is the school that is the locus of the kind of professional learning that can change thinking in practice.

The network doesn't bypass the school. It works by strengthening the school—that is, by strengthening the within-school learning community to ensure that schools have the clear and defensible learning focus, skills for collaborative inquiry, and leadership (formal and informal) to influence professional learning. This is what we described earlier as the upload/download relationship between the schools and the network (represented by the up and down "white" arrows in Figure 2.2). Individuals—either directly or through the artifacts and processes they create—are the boundary spanners that link the school to the network and vice versa. Throughout this book, you will see multiple examples of this upload/download relationship. You will see it described in terms of the work of both administrators and teacher leaders who move back and forth between the school and network in an iterative and purposeful way, always with an eye toward creating, supporting, and strengthening the kinds of within-school communities that behave as learning organizations.

Figure 2.2 Key Enablers of Teacher Learning—Professional Knowledge Creation and Sharing

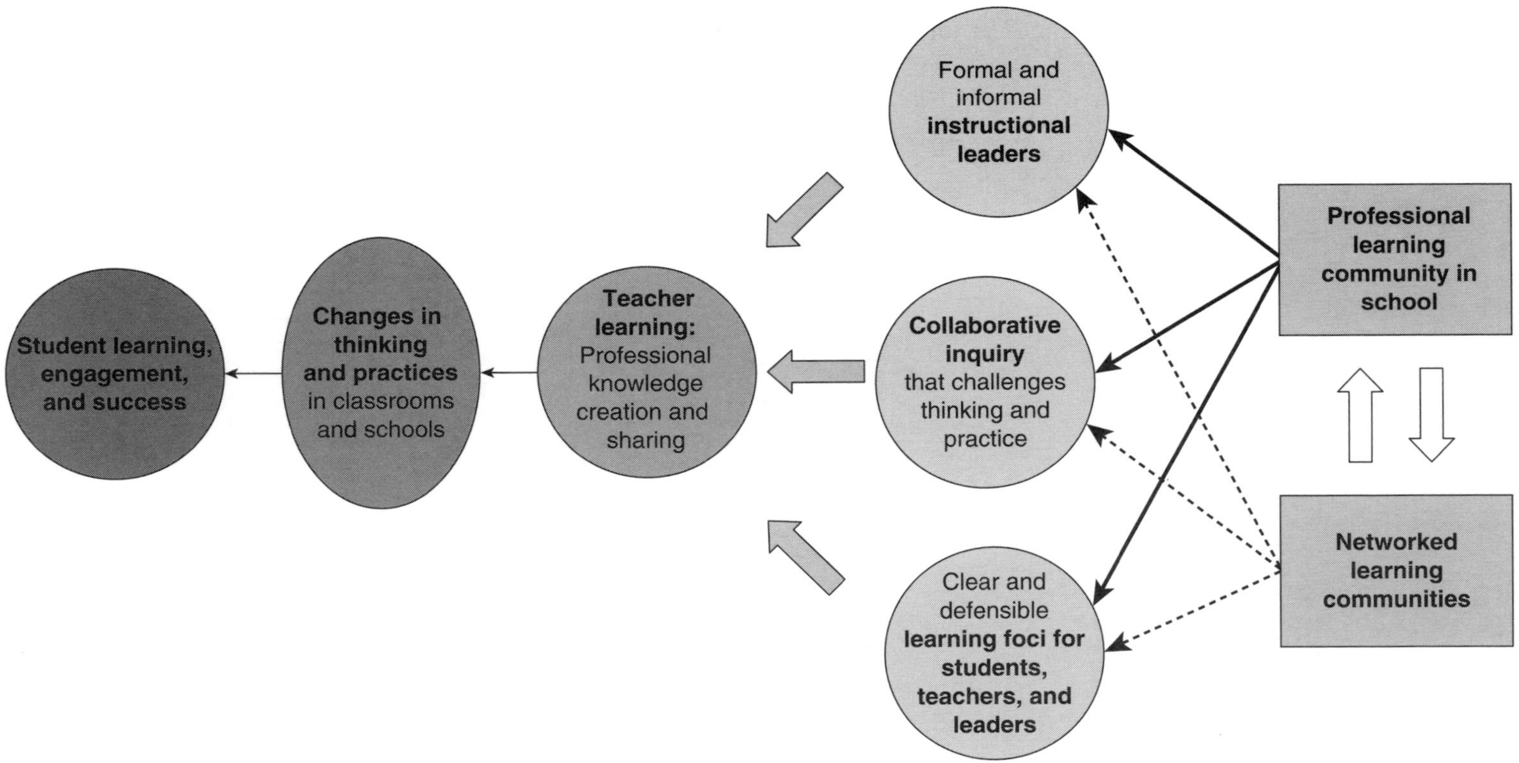

Focused Professional Learning in Schools

Figure 2.3 magnifies the within-school learning and recognizes that these enablers are not always in place in schools. It highlights the interrelationships among the key enablers and draws attention to the need to build capacity in the key enablers for focused collaborative inquiry that challenges thinking and practice and focused instructional leadership to be enacted in every school. This is not capacity building in a global sense. It is building capacity in the right kinds of enablers to move towards *focused* professional learning and *focused* changes in classroom practice in each school to influence school improvement in specific defined areas.

The high-leverage elements of "relationships," "collaboration," and "inquiry" come together in the concept that we describe as "collaborative inquiry that challenges thinking and practice." Similarly, the impactful components of both formal and informal leadership coalesce in the notion of "instructional leadership." Our intent in this book is to unpack these research-based and empirically validated enablers of focused professional learning and illustrate what it means to build, support, and sustain effective NLCs.

Time for Reflection

Think about your school in relation to the following questions:

Do you have a forum for professional knowledge creation and sharing?

What is your school's learning focus for students and how is that influencing the learning focus for teachers and leaders?

What (if any) collaborative inquiry has the staff (or PLC) undertaken together? How was it related to your learning focus?

Who are the informal leaders in the school?

Figure 2.3   Building Capacity for Focused Professional Learning

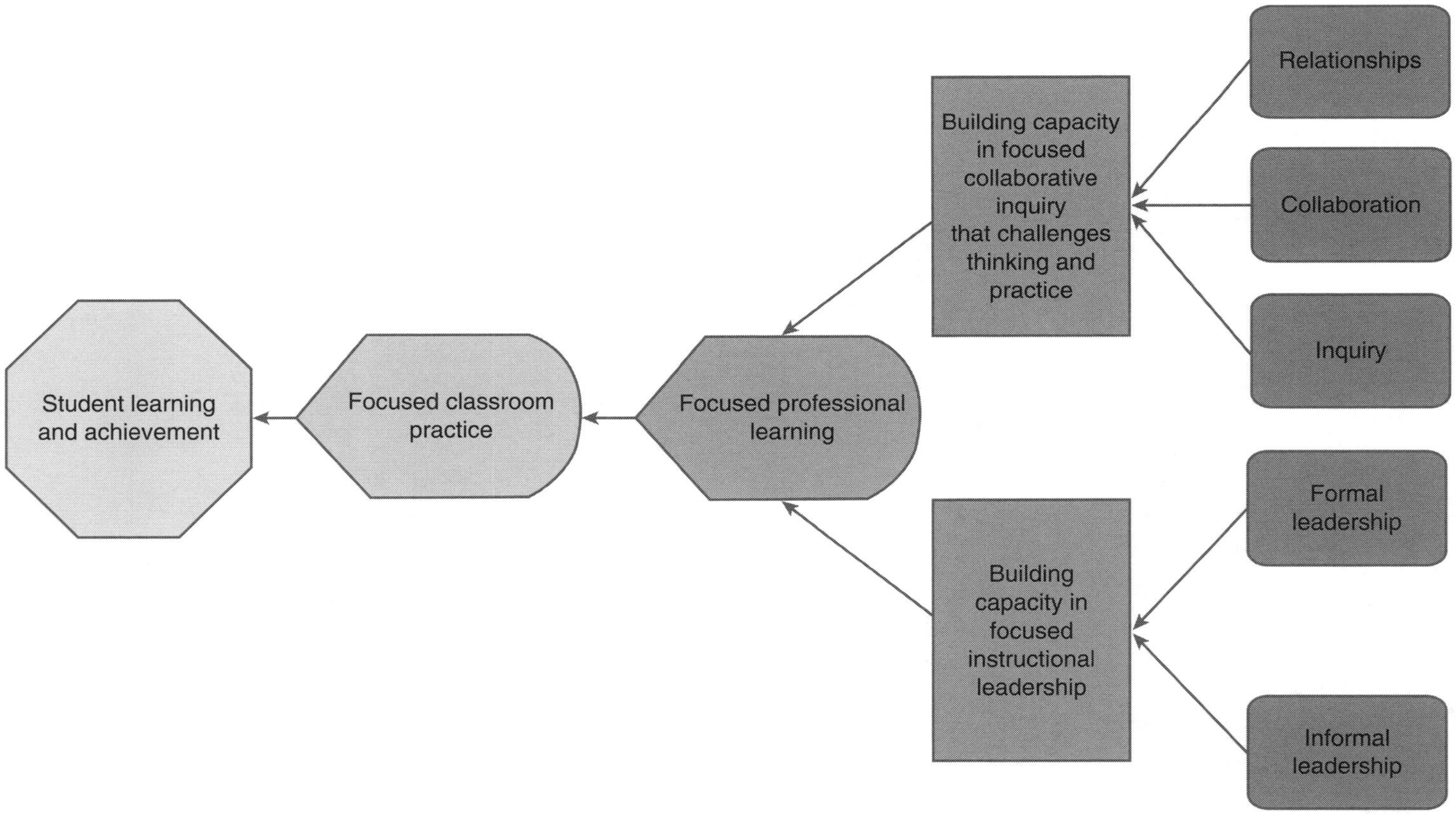

3

Establishing a Clear and Defensible Focus

Carl had an impression that most of the schools in Joan's family of schools shared a common issue with literacy. He wanted to create a forum for the school leaders to talk through their context and school achievement so they could start to decide whether they did indeed share a focus.

Carl asked all of the principals in the area to bring their assessment results to the next meeting so that they could work together to identify areas of mutual interest and do some joint planning. Carl asked Joan to start the conversation. Joan described her initial disappointment with the school results, because there was no improvement in her school's scores despite the continuous efforts from her staff. She explained that her school's PLC (professional learning community) all agreed that reading was a problem area, but that since their efforts had not been fruitful, she was not sure what to do next.

Charles (principal of Braggard, a K–6 school) echoed Joan's story and explained that he was primarily concerned with the literacy scores in Grades 4–6. When his school leadership team reviewed the results, it had identified that reading comprehension continued to be an issue. But, he added, since he had introduced the reading block in his school, the team did notice a moderate improvement in the results compared with two years ago.

Laila (principal of Winston Elementary) said, "My school's literacy scores are actually pretty good. We are above the district average and we are meeting our annual targets. We have been really focusing on literacy for the last five years. Unfortunately, our mathematics results are not as impressive—we are below the district average and we have not met our school improvement targets."

Elsie (the principal of West Chelsy) stated, "I wish I could find one area to concentrate on. We have been working on both literacy and numeracy initiatives for the last two years and I don't think our kids can really do the work that gets tested in the statewide tests because of their low levels when they arrive in the school. Our teachers are really using the most innovative strategies. We have had some good experts working with us and they have all told me that they are impressed with my teachers."

Rita (principal of Whitecrest) echoed Elsie's situation and said that her school's literacy scores were worse than the math scores despite the teachers' efforts using new strategies that were introduced to them through a literacy specialist at the district.

Rikard (the principal of Rayrist) said, "My school's situation is similar to that of Joan and Charles. But I am not sure how much you can do when you have a normal distribution. It is what it is supposed to be. I expect to have some students who are doing well, some who are doing poorly, and most of them are average—and that is what I am seeing."

Carl listened carefully as the principals exchanged stories highlighting the efforts being made in their schools and the common drive toward improved learning. He joined the discussion to summarize the information shared in the group, and in so doing identified a common set of needs between the schools. He added that he knew literacy was a common issue in the area when he reviewed the district results. Reading comprehension, in particular, appeared to be a common issue amongst the schools. He continued to think out loud and suggested that if the members of the group worked together in the service of improvement, they could collectively achieve greater success than working individually.

All of the principals agreed with Carl's idea of doing something collegial in a supportive atmosphere to target the issue of literacy in schools. The group articulated the potential advantages of having a supportive network of professionals who were all investing their efforts to improve the literacy levels in their schools. Although the principals all expressed a desire to be involved, they also wanted more details on how the group would work together. Carl's response was explicit: since the group's participation would be completely voluntary, the group would have to decide how it could best work together.

FOCUS FOREMOST

Educators are action people who define themselves by what they do. Most of them did not choose this profession to be armchair quarterbacks or commentators. They chose it because there is no place they'd rather be than in the game. But the action orientation of education has meant that they are often victims of shotgun approaches to school improvement. They fire, watch the buckshot spread, and hope they hit something. The seduction of this approach/ solution is that it is loaded with activity, and if activity were a proxy for improvement things would be fine. Unfortunately, levels of activity hold no direct promise of improvement. In fact, there is a good chance of ending up in an "activity trap" focused on doing, where the activity may be ineffective, or even counterproductive.

> *Activity traps* are those "doings" that, while well intentioned, are not truly needs based and have the effect of diverting resources (both human and material) away from where they are most necessary.

The troubling nature of activity traps is that you don't know when you're in one. The combination of good intentions and hard work constructs a convincing delusion. We had occasion to spend time in a school not that long ago that had a showcase anti-bullying program in place. It comprised a dazzling array of dispute-resolution mechanisms from peer mediators to conflict resolution rooms. Only one thing was missing—a bullying problem in the first place. Simply put, there was no evidence of a bullying problem that required remediation. As it turned out, several staff had attended an anti-bullying workshop on the district's mandatory professional development day. The guest

> *Initiativitis* (n): The disease of the initiative.
>
> *Symptoms:* Typically include the unexpected arrival of a new three-ring materials binder with multiple colored tabs.
>
> *Prognosis:* Unless treated, results in an activity trap and stalled school improvement progress.
>
> *Prescription:* Can be prevented by a carefully chosen, needs-based improvement focus.

speaker was captivating and the program materials were readily available and cheap. And so they were off . . . right into an activity trap, victims of the disease we might call "initiativitis."

Economists talk about "opportunity cost"—what is lost when the most valuable alternative is not implemented. This notion explains why "initiativitis" is such a dangerous disease. When you're in an activity trap, what you are doing keeps you from doing other things. There's somewhere else you can't be, and that somewhere is precisely the place you need to be. The operative word here is *need*. Establishing need is about focus. It is about aiming before you fire—though this doesn't mean that you never fire; it just means you aim first! It is the antithesis of the shotgun approach to improvement.

Carl wanted to ensure that the principals reflected strategically on the current information they each had about their schools to identify an explicit shared focus before deciding on activities.

He explained that the network effort must be focused and useful for the schools so that it did not become one giant "activity trap" that drained resources without making a difference. He asked the group what they might do to ensure that they did indeed share a common, needs-based focus.

Charles: I think that we should review our school assessment results together to figure out the priority issue that should be our focus.

Elsie: That is a good idea, but that is a lot of work and we already know that we all have issues with literacy. Carl even said so earlier.

Laila: Well, not all of us. I have a math issue in my school. Our literacy scores are fine.

Rita: That is true, but the rest of us are struggling with literacy in our schools.

Rikard: Maybe not struggling, but just wanting to do better.

Joan: What about the item-level analysis?

Charles: That's a good idea. We can use the standards-based report from the Grade 6 literacy assessment to make decisions about the kinds of professional development we need.

Joan: Or Grade 3—they have the same categories.

Rita: Our school had a series of workshops on that last year. The standards-based reports are part of the package that we receive from the evaluation unit. You should already have them in print form. The item-level reports give the results grouped by strand, topic, and concept. So that when you take the time to really look at them, it really helps you realize what exact areas—skills or knowledge—are weak in the school.

         In my school, we had all the teachers spend three half days in a workshop where the expert guided us through the steps. I still have the workshop guidebook and it is very helpful. We could streamline the guide to help us look at our own results and figure out where we need to focus our efforts to help the students in reading comprehension. It could take less time since we already have a kind of focused approach.

Joan: That sounds great.

Charles: Yeah. But did it have an impact on the school?

Rita: That's a tough one. Well, no—but I think that's because after the workshops, we really could not follow up immediately. Last year, we identified that "making inferences" in reading comprehension was a big problem. But we really could not do anything about it because I had to deal with a teacher leaving and a lot of our kids are ESL so some of the teachers have been doing PD on teaching ESL students. I guess we just dropped the ball.

Joan: I like the idea of having a guide that we can use with our staff to look at the item-level reports so that we can figure out what the biggest issues are. What if Rita sends us the guide and we all commit to using it with our staff to find out what the major issues are?

Charles: What if we all do it with our Grade 3 literacy results and then meet in three weeks to report back to each other?

The rest of the team agreed. Carl was very pleased with the outcome of the meeting. He felt that the direction and process of the group were very positive.

Carl is responsible for the group of schools and wants to give each of his schools the attention they need and deserve. But meeting the needs of all his schools is a challenge because his portfolio of responsibilities has him stretched very thin. Despite his best intentions, he often finds himself being more reactive than proactive in his relationship with his schools. Supporting the group of schools to work together as a network makes him feel that he has the opportunity to be more intentional in supporting their improvement efforts. Carl also feels that, as a formal leader in the system, this network will be a valuable learning opportunity for him. Of course, he would still need to deal with the exigencies of individual schools on issues like resource allocation, staffing, students with particular issues, and the like. But a learning network—especially a focused one—could provide an efficient organizational form for targeting his school improvement pressure and support.

Psychologists are fond of studying experts in the hopes of finding out what it is that makes them so good at what they do. They study everything from expert chess players to expert golfers to expert musicians—and yes, expert teachers as well. The idea is that learning more about what contributes to expertise can provide some kind of blueprint to help others get better too. A number of common characteristics that define experts, regardless of domain, are relevant here. Experts are generally faster than novices—something that might seem obvious—but they are not faster than novices in every phase of activity. Experts spend significantly more time than novices analyzing the demands of a given situation, on what we call the problem-identification stage (Glaser & Chi, 1988). When novices are already well on their way to "doing," experts are spending their time analyzing and learning. They use this time to represent the problems or challenges at a deeper level and really try to understand all of the relevant issues before they make decisions about what to do. In other words, experts spend more time than novices on "aiming." When experts encounter difficulties along the way, they have many options and alternatives to draw on, because they have spent the time in analysis and preparation. Novices, on the other hand, face obstacles and "hit the wall," sometimes even giving up, because they have no foundation for adjustments or shifts.

EVIDENCE-BASED FOCUS

In an earlier book, *Leading Schools in a Data-Rich World: Harnessing Data for School Improvement* (Earl & Katz, 2006), and the accompanying facilitator's guide (Earl, Katz, & Ben Jaafar, 2008), we described the central role of evidence in the school improvement enterprise. In particular, we pointed out the way in which evidence informs the priority-setting process. Earlier in this chapter, we cautioned against the dangers of activity traps. Evidence keeps you out of activity traps by making sure that the work of improvement is aimed—that it is needs-based and therefore focused.

We have watched the priority-setting pendulum swing from personal supposition (I "think" we need . . .) to data driven (our data tells us that . . .). While there has been a shift in school improvement toward a consideration of evidence, a (perhaps) unintended consequence of this shift has been that tacit knowledge—teachers' beliefs based on their personal experience, training, and history—has been dismissed as unimportant or, even worse, as an impediment. But as we argued in *Leading Schools*, there is no objective truth to be "found" in data. Data don't "tell" us anything; they are benign. The meaning that comes from data comes from interpretation, and interpretation is a human endeavor that involves a mix of insights from evidence and the tacit knowledge that the group brings to the discussion. Interpreting evidence includes establishing hypotheses, testing them, and ultimately making sense of it all. This is a collective thinking process that is subject to all of the same cognitive biases that plague most of our sense-making efforts. Cognitive biases refer to the psychological propensity of human beings to preserve and conserve existing beliefs by seeking out and finding ways to move towards confirmation and away from contradictions. We will have much more to say about cognitive biases later. After all, they are the reason that real new learning—true conceptual change—is so difficult. For now, what is important is to understand that beliefs are the filters through which individuals and groups engage with evidence and interpret data. Existing beliefs are an essential ingredient for imbuing data with meaning.

Later on, in Chapter 6, we'll describe how creating new knowledge is a process of co-construction by which internal beliefs and external evidence are considered in relation to each other. This is at the heart of what's involved in determining a needs-based focus. The process begins by tapping into tacit knowledge, by engaging in a hypothesis generation exercise and recasting "what we know" into "what we *think* we know." Determining priority areas—establishing focus—is a combination of belief and data. Instead of suspending beliefs in the service of data or adamantly defending unsubstantiated beliefs, the conversation is a forum for examining both and making the interrelationship explicit.

In *Leading Schools in a Data-Rich World*, we used a painting metaphor for using data for improvement. Artists are always engaging with data—with the colors, textures, and images that they observe and investigate, and to which they respond. They use their talent to decide what to emphasize and how to communicate a mood and a message to the audience. Educators can capture the myriad and changeable images that matter about a school and present these images to a range of audiences as the basis for ongoing decision making. Sometimes the paintings are completed individually, as teachers or leaders work on their own. In other cases, educators work in teams to create a collage or a mural of their thinking and their work. In all cases, they draw on many sources of information to construct a coherent and distinctive image of where they are now, where they want to be in the future, and how they might go about bridging the gap. Finally, educators paint many pictures, not just one, with different purposes, audiences, and issues to consider. Most painters—even those who appear to be undisciplined and random in their actions—go through a great deal of thinking and planning before they ever begin to paint. Once they have a notion of the content, mood, and image they hope to capture, they rely on having well-developed technical skills to select their palette and execute the process of painting, all the while making adjustments, changing ideas, and rethinking their vision. Educational teams can follow the same principles when they appeal to data in their improvement process.

When it comes to establishing a focus, the goal is to identify the most urgent student learning needs by tapping into tacit knowledge as the source of possible hypotheses. On the basis of the group's tacit knowledge, what do members think are the student learning needs and what do they think they know about the various factors that are germane to them? From there, they move to a third question—what evidence do they have (or could they get) to inform their hypotheses? In the painting metaphor, we use the concept of indicator categories—broad-based groupings of types of evidence—to approximate the colors on the artist's palette. Indicator categories include things like "student achievement," "student demographics," "teaching and assessment practices," and so on (see *Leading Schools in a Data-Rich World* for many more examples). Within each category, a range of possible data sources exist that speak to the particular category. For example, "student achievement" can be informed by standardized assessments, in-class work, report card results, and so on. Likewise, "teaching and assessment practices" can include data on instructional strategies employed in the classroom, classroom management practices, assessment practices, and instructional time and environment.

Joan returned to her school enthusiastic about attending to her school's data to identify their focus based on 'hard' evidence.

She found the e-mail from Rita including an attachment, the promised guide. After reading through the guide and talking with Rita on the phone about some of her questions, Joan scheduled a half-day session with her PLC team. As preparation for the meeting, she instructed her PLC team members to each develop a hypothesis about why they were not making gains in reading comprehension in the school.

The PLC team (made up of Raymond, a long-standing Grade 3 teacher; Leslie, a Grade 2 teacher who had expertise in English strategies; Meriem, a Grade 6 teacher with a mathematics education background; and Leigh, a newly qualified Grade 4 teacher) met. Joan summarized the events that had led to the meeting and then invited each member to put up one of their hypotheses about reading comprehension. She wrote these on the board.

1. *Boys are struggling with reading comprehension more than girls.*

2. *ESL students are bringing down the average literacy score of the whole school.*

3. *The students are doing well in understanding the text, but they are struggling with making inferences because we only have time in the year to get the students to that level of understanding.*

4. *The students are struggling with understanding the text even though we spend all our time on it. This means that they can't do well on the higher-level skills.*

5. *We have made improvements in reading comprehension, but we are still under the district average so it is not being celebrated.*

Joan: We seem to have some differences in opinion about what is happening with our literacy results.

Meriem: Yes, but we all agree that this school needs to work on our reading comprehension.

Raymond: That is true in this room, but I don't know that some of our colleagues would agree. I know a couple who would argue for a focus on writing rather than reading.

Joan: Well, I think that this process will help build a shared understanding if we can communicate it to the rest of the staff using the numbers.

Raymond: I agree. I think that the data will be very persuasive in giving us a common direction.

Meriem: So where do we start?

Joan: Well, we just did. The first step was to identify what we think we know about our focus. We now need to figure out how to test our hypotheses using the data that we have.

Meriem: Great. So how do we do that?

Joan: We need to consider our indicators. One of the principals in another school sent me the table that she used with her staff and it worked really well with them. So I thought we could use it. The first thing that we need to do is get a common understanding of the terminology, and then work through the table.

The team sifted through the assessment data to test the five hypotheses. Members spent most of the half-day session agreeing on their common responses by examining the assessment reports and the results. Only forty minutes were left in the half-day session by the time they had completed the following table together.

Hypothesis (I think that…)	Indicator (What is the data that I can use to check my hypothesis?)	Evidence (I can see that…)	Given this evidence we would say that …
1. Boys are struggling with reading comprehension more than girls.	Gender Overall reading scores	*Males:* 42 percent of boys met standards, 33 percent of boys approached standards, and 25 percent of boys were below standards *Females:* 46 percent of girls met standards, 35 percent of girls approached standards, and 19 percent of girls were below standards.	The difference between the scores of the girls and boys is not very large. There are 6 percent more boys than girls below standard. We don't have a big issue with a difference in achievement between girls and boys, but we want to keep monitoring the results to make sure the difference does not increase.
2. ESL students are bringing down the average literacy score of the whole school.	English as a Foreign Language (EFL) Non-EFL (students whose mother language is English) Overall reading scores	*EFL:* 41 percent of EFL students met standards, 30 percent of EFL students approached standards, and 29 percent of EFL students were below standards *Non-EFL:* There is no data for just these students *All students:* 45 percent of students met standards, 35 percent of students approached standards, and 20 percent of students were below standards.	More students who have English as their mother tongue are approaching and meeting standards than EFL students. There are 9 percent more EFL students not meeting standards than the overall percentage for all the students. We have a small issue with foreign students not doing as well as native language students.

(Continued)

(Continued)

Hypothesis (I think that . . .)	Indicator (What is the data that I can use to check my hypothesis?)	Evidence (I can see that . . .)	Given this evidence we would say that . . .
3. The students are doing well in understanding the text, but they are struggling with making inferences because we only have time in the year to get the students to that level of understanding.	Reading Skills 1: Understanding explicit information in the text Reading Skills 2: understanding implicit information in the text Reading Skills 3: making connections between reading and own knowledge	Reading Skills 1: 83 percent of students met or were above the standards (Note: all multiple-choice questions) Reading Skills 2: 37 percent of students met or were above the standards (Note: 50 percent multiple-choice questions and 50 percent written response) Reading Skills 3: 10 percent of students met or were above the standards (Note: All written response questions)	In order to better understand the overall achievement, we need to realize that each Reading Skills category has a different weight for the overall passing score. RS1 is worth 30 percent, RS2 is worth 40 percent, and RS3 is worth 20 percent. The students need more support in understanding implicit information in the text (RS2) if we want the achievement to increase. Most of the students did not pass in the written response questions asking about making connections (RS3). This could be a problem with writing or the reading skill.
4. The students are struggling with understanding the text, even	Time spent on understanding the text Reading Skills 1: Understanding	Same evidence as in previous cell. No data on time spent in class on each reading skill	Most of the students (83 percent) are doing very well on understanding the text (RS1).

Hypothesis (I think that...)	Indicator (What is the data that I can use to check my hypothesis?)	Evidence (I can see that...)	Given this evidence we would say that ...
though we spend all our time on it. This means that they can't do well on the higher-level skills.	explicit information in the text *Reading Skills 2:* understanding implicit information in the text *Reading Skills 3:* making connections between reading and own knowledge		Students are struggling with the higher level skills, but not because they don't understand the text.
5. We have made improvements in reading comprehension, but we are still under the district average so it is not being celebrated.	Overall reading score (this year) Overall reading score (last year) Overall reading scores (two years ago)	*This year:* 45 percent of students met standards, 35 percent of students approached standards, and 20 percent of students were below standards. *Last year:* 46 percent of students met standards, 30 percent of students approached standards, and 24 percent of students were below standards. *Two years ago:* 47 percent of students met standards, 26 percent of students approached standards, and 27 percent of students were below standards.	We have not made gains in the percentage of students meeting standards. We have fewer students below the standards and more students approaching the standards. In two years, 9 percent more students are approaching standards. The improvements we have made seem to be targeting the lowest achieving students. It is possible that the students we are getting are changing. We need to keep monitoring these data.

Raymond: This table is pretty simple now. Hard to believe that it took all the work that we put in.

Meriem: Well, we certainly did do a lot of discussing to come up with these little bits of information about our hypotheses.

Joan: I like the way it is set up because it makes discussing the hypotheses a lot easier.

Raymond: So is it time to start that discussion?

Joan: I think so.

The team discussed the last column. It concluded that the school did need to focus its energy on promoting Reading Skills 2, understanding implicit information in the text, and Reading Skills 3, making connections between reading and own knowledge. It noted that the school did not need to focus its attention on ESL or male learners. Finally, the team acknowledged that over the last three years there had been an improvement in the percentage of students who approached standards—an improvement that would not be noticeable in the overall reporting of the school.

Joan felt like she had made a major breakthrough in understanding her school's needs and was relieved to have a direction for improvement. She now knew what to promote and where to allocate the literacy resources so that her school would have a better chance of increasing the number of students who were achieving the standards. In short, Joan had an evidence-informed school focus!

FROM A SCHOOL FOCUS TO A NETWORK FOCUS

Establishing a networked learning community (NLC) and agreeing about a focus are just the beginning of a journey of exploration and learning. The participants will find themselves in unfamiliar territory of working and learning with others in new ways. Moving from PLCs in schools to networked PLCs is a major shift for educators, who typically do not have a lot of opportunities to work with others outside their own school, or experience in doing so. A common focus is the glue that binds schools in a NLC together. Without a common needs-based focus, there is no impetus for schools to work together. Our research has found that the kind of network foci that impact on classroom practice, and in turn on student achievement, are foci that are *right* for each school, *understood* by all the members, and *shared* amongst the schools (Katz, Earl, Ben Jaafar et al., 2008).

At the next area meeting, Carl wanted to establish an evidence-based network focus that was shared by all the schools. He invited the principals to share the results of the exploration of their school literacy results and their school focus.

Rita started the conversation. She reported that her school team had found substantial improvement over the last three years in her school's results for understanding explicit information, or Reading Skills 1. The results went from 50 percent of students meeting or exceeding expectations in this skill to 90 percent. Unfortunately, the same improvement had not been observed in the other reading skills. Her team discussed the results and agreed that the new strategies it had been promoting in classes focused on understanding explicit text; the team would now need to focus on student skills in making inferences.

Elsie reported that her school results were so low that her team had decided to bypass looking at the reading skills results individually. It only looked at the overall results from the last three years, and there was no improvement in the overall reading and writing scores. The scores hovered at around 38 percent of students meeting the standards. She reported that her school team had agreed that, since it needed help in all areas, it would follow the network group's consensus.

Rikard reported that, overall, the students were having difficulty with inference and making connections. Only 39 percent of the students were meeting or exceeding expectations in these two strands. His team also noted that the girls in the school did better on the open-response questions than the boys. As a result, there were 10 percent more girls than boys who met or exceeded standards on making connections, or Reading Skills 3.

Laila reported that her initial impressions were confirmed. The literacy scores in her school were high. The results were between 70 and 87 percent of all students meeting or exceeding standards in all reading skills. Unfortunately, her math results were not as encouraging. Only 29 percent of the students at Winston met the standards in Patterning and Algebra; and only 15 percent of them met the standards in Data Management and Probability. She was very disappointed to learn that her teachers were essentially skimming over the Algebra curriculum and barely addressing the Data curriculum.

Joan reported that her school results indicated that, although there had been improvements in the students' reading skills over the last three years, the students were below the standards line. She explained that her school results were particularly low in Reading Skills 2 and 3. About 45 percent of her students were reaching the standards overall. But when they looked at the scores by reading skills, about 40 percent and 10 percent respectively were reaching the standards in Reading Skills 2 and 3. The only reason they had 45 percent of the students passing was because most students did well on Reading Skills 1, which was worth 30 percent of the test. Her team was confident in its decision to focus on inference strategies to improve student achievement. That direction would really focus on Reading Skills 2, which made up 40 percent of the literacy assessment.

Charles summarized what he heard and noted that, with the exception of Laila and Elsie, there was direct evidence of a common need amongst the schools—inference strategies in reading comprehension.

Elsie: I am happy with a focus on reading comprehension and making inferences.

Charles: I realize that your team agreed to follow the focus of this group, but I think that it is important for you and your team to work through the details of your results to really make sure that this focus fits according to your data.

Elsie: It was just that we had so much data so, even with the guide, it just seemed like it would take a lot of time that we don't have.

Joan: I had to book half a day and we took all the time I booked. We could have used more time because we had more questions at the end. We could go through another round looking at different parts of the data now. But the guide does help you focus your attention. If we did not spend the time, we would not have seen the possibilities for change that we can actually work on. Once we started, my teachers found the conversation gave them some direction for change, instead of just feeling overwhelmed.

Rita: The guide really does help. It makes sifting through the data manageable.

Elsie: Okay, I will book half a day with the PLC, then, and see what happens.

Rikard: I am happy with making inferences in reading as a focus. It serves our needs as well. If I can get support from the team, I would prefer to work together on something we all need than apart on one thing that I need.

Laila: Well, it sounds like I really don't fit in because I need to work on numeracy in my school.

Rikard: I would like to be inclusive, but I really think that would divide our focus.

Rita: I have to agree with Rikard. I don't think that we can do both. That is not a focus.

Laila: I think that I really just need to work with a group of people whose school is in the same boat as mine.

Carl: I think that is what a focus is for. There is no mandatory piece here. If the network does not fit your needs, then it is not the right network for you. It seems to me that I am hearing agreement with respect to a common student learning need across all the schools except Winston Elementary. So, if we take Winston out of the equation, we have a sensible learning network focused on making inferences as a reading comprehension skill.

Joan: Okay, so we will form a network of schools that is organized around a shared student learning need—inference and making connections in reading comprehension.

Rita: I like it.

Charles: I can stand behind it and so can my school.

Elsie: I will coordinate a half-day meeting with my literacy team next week and we can look at the reading comprehension results. I anticipate the same results.

Laila: I just want to say that, even though this did not work out for me, I do think that this was helpful. I now know the real weak spots in mathematics in my school, which will serve as our new focus.

Carl: Laila, we should talk tomorrow about other schools that might be a better fit for a network that is focusing on mathematics.

Laila: That sounds good.

Joan: Now that we know what we want to work on, I think that we need to strike while the iron is hot.

Elsie: Let's meet in two weeks at West Chelsy. This way we won't lose focus on what we are really about—students! I will host the next meeting and make sure that we have space and refreshments. And I will have my results looked at by then.

Carl: The district will cover the refreshments.

Elsie: Great!

Once the group confirmed the date and time of the meeting next week, Carl asked the principals to send any agenda items to Elsie, since she was the host.

Time for Reflection

What do you believe is the most urgent need for the students in your school?

What are your hypotheses about what is influencing the need?

What data could you use to test these hypotheses?

Look at the data to confirm, challenge, or refine your hypotheses.

What does this exercise suggest as a specific focus for improvement of student learning?

4

Collaborative Inquiry to Challenge Thinking and Practice

THE IMPORTANCE OF RELATIONSHIPS

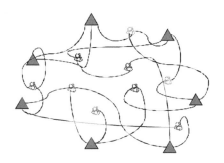

M adeline Church and her colleagues (2002) have suggested the image of a physical net as a metaphor for the anatomy of networked learning (see above figure). Essentially, nets are made out of threads and knots. Threads, tied together in knots, provide the structural integrity of the net; this is what makes the net "work," so to speak. In the networked learning community (NLC) model, the threads represent the relationships between the partner entities (the schools and the people who represent them), while the knots are the substance of collaboration. The nature of the knots can vary, and we will have much more to say about the different faces of collaboration later because collaboration, along with inquiry and relationships, is a key contributor to that critical "enabler" of professional learning that we have called *focused collaborative inquiry that challenges thinking and practice.* But for now, the focus is on the threads, on the relationships.

It makes sense that networks operate on linkages and interdependencies. But, as researchers Allen and Cherrey (2000) argue, we have been misguided in our attempts to understand the connections through organizational structure. Instead, it is helpful to view the relationships *themselves* as the connections. Relationships are what makes it possible for a network to knit together. The network needs to provide the mechanisms to support the relationships in the service of sustainability and vitality.

The argument that relationships are the "connective tissue" of networks finds support in the notion of social capital. Social capital is developed through social interaction that allows people to work together in the service of achievements that exceed what any of them could accomplish alone (Halverson, 2003). In practice, networks use social capital to create a common language, channels for communicating and disseminating information to one another, knowledge about network members' expertise, and widespread readiness to trust another (Smith & Wohlstetter, 2001).

Relationships are strengthened as trust grows (Church et al., 2002). Trust—or what Bryk and Schneider (2002) call "relational trust"—has been found to be a particularly strong facilitator of professional community, and is a necessary condition for developing the kind of professional commitment that contributes to school improvement. This conception of trust goes beyond that of goodwill and friendship, though such "companion trust" (Newell & Swan, 2000) is certainly essential. It extends to include respect for each others' dignity and ideas, belief in each other's competence, and a confidence in each other's integrity to put students first (Bryk & Schneider, 2002). Relational trust focuses on establishing shared expectations for the work together.

The antecedents and consequences of relational patterns in networks are not always easy to tease apart. It is a classic chicken/egg problem. Lieberman and Grolnick (1996) found that trusting relationships amongst network members led to a powerful participation effect of working with people who had different orientations to building knowledge. That said, it is through working and reflecting together intentionally that trust grows and relationships, in turn, are strengthened; trust does not build itself (Church et al., 2002). Activities that can produce trust as a consequence may also require it as an antecedent.

So where does one begin? How do you penetrate the cycle of needing relational trust to be able to work together in ways that breed relational trust? Strong threads are necessary for good knots, while good knots are necessary for strong threads. This is a difficult challenge—one made even more difficult by the (almost guaranteed) likelihood that the absence of existing relationships will be offered up as the most popular impediment to intentionally building learning networks, a finding supported by our own research into the challenges of scaling up NLCs as a district reform strategy (Katz, 2007). In other words, beliefs about relationships can be gatekeepers, as people assess the possible advantages and pitfalls in these new relationships and decide whether or not to move forward.

Given all of this, it is important to be explicit about certain key dimensions of the relationship challenge. First, relational trust won't just arrive out of thin air; it requires intentional cultivation. The thread–knot relationship is iterative; threads grow out of knots (the collaborative activities) as much as they precede them, so we need to get going on the knots. Second, while relationships are an important beginning and a sound investment from a cultural perspective, they are not ends in and of themselves in the context of learning networks. A preoccupation with relationships as "ends" carries all the making of an activity trap—a focus on the doing but not on the outcomes. Third, the kind of relational trust we are talking about here is professional, not personal. Network members need to trust one another to help them do their professional best, not to be the guardians of their closely held family secrets, for example. And finally, relational trust is not an all or nothing phenomenon. The trick is to cultivate enough relational trust to cross the threshold that is the gateway to collaboration. That is, there needs to be just enough thread to tie a knot because the knot, in turn, will strengthen the thread.

The question at this point becomes one of developing a strategy for building the beginnings of relationships, for cultivating enough relational trust to feel as if the potential network members are in it together. When people are asked to explain what constitutes the foundation of successful relationships, they typically subscribe to one of two popular, yet opposing, clichés. The first is that "birds of feather flock together"—that similarity lies at the heart of relationships that work. The second is that "opposites attract"—that relationships are created through difference. Psychologists have studied both phenomena and, as it turns out, empirical validation rests with the former (Passer, Smith, Atkinson, Mitchell, & Muir, 2005). Commonalities, rather than differences, lie at the root of relationships that are ultimately judged to be successful. And it is commonality—commonality in the school-based learning focus—that gives NLCs the relationship kick-start they require.

Carl wanted to create opportunities for the group of principals to start building trust in the group and for distributed leadership.

Before leaving the room, Carl explained that he would no longer facilitate or lead any more meetings. He asked the principals to consider the group's organization and leadership. He explained that he needed their decision about the group with enough detail that would enable him to make the group official at the district level.

The principals remained, and Elsie suggested that Carl and Joan continue to lead the group because they had started the network. Joan's ears perked up at Elsie's suggestion, but before she could share her feelings of discomfort with the suggestion, Rita reminded the group that Carl had stated he would not lead the group.

Elsie:	Really! Why wouldn't he?
Rita:	Sounds like he wants to document it for the district and let us do the work.
Rikard:	That is not what I understood. He said he did not want to lead the group, but I got the impression that he would continue to participate.
Charles:	But as the district leader, isn't it his job to lead school principals?
Rikard:	Yes, but we distribute leadership in our schools, so it makes sense that he lets us self-direct for our learning group. I don't know that he is even sure how he will continue to participate, but let's make a plan on how we are going to work together assuming he won't take on any official role in the group.
Joan:	I agree. I think that he wants us to decide for ourselves. I get the sense that he does want to be a part of our network, but not lead it formally.
Elsie:	Okay. In that case, I really feel that Joan should be the group leader because she started this thing.
Rikard:	Joan, how do you feel about it?
Joan:	Not good. Look, I don't know much about networks and I did not really start anything—I called Carl for help when I realized that our school's efforts were not as effective as I wanted them to be. This is where the call landed. I like the way we have been working.
Rikard:	Okay. But I don't think that network leadership is about knowing the answers. To be honest, I think it is more about knowing how to ask the right questions and how to ask for help at the right time. You have shown that you can do that already.
Elsie:	The leader will also organize meetings, make sure that we follow up on action points, and do the usual organizational things for a group. We need someone to keep records, make agendas, and guide the group.
Rikard:	Okay. And we all do that in our jobs so we all know how to do that.
Rita:	What about it, Joan?

Joan:	I am not comfortable doing it on my own. I will do it with someone.
Elsie:	I just feel overwhelmed right now. So I can't help that way.
Charles:	I will do it with you. We can share the leadership responsibilities. If one of us takes charge of managerial duties and the other takes care of leading the group through the thinking pieces during the meetings and following up on decisions, it could be more manageable. What do we think of co-leaders?
Joan:	Yes, but I would prefer to continue having the group making the decisions together.
Charles:	I think that we all agree on that. We still need leadership to guide us through the processes.
Joan:	Okay.

The group finalized its decision. Joan agreed that she would write up brief notes documenting the members' decision and Charles would edit them. The organization and leadership notes would be sent to the group by the end of the next week for comments and then given to Carl at the next meeting. In the meantime, the principals agreed that they could confidently promote the focus within their schools.

FROM INQUIRY TO AN INQUIRY HABIT OF MIND

Building capacity for inquiry as a practice of knowledge creation requires effort because it is hard work to move beyond natural preservation and conservation propensities. Like any new and complex skill, inquiry takes time and deliberate practice to develop. But for inquiry to truly be effective, it needs to become a way of doing business, a way of thinking, a *habit of mind*, rather than a discrete event. The definition of a habit is a settled tendency of practice. Habits are things people do both frequently and automatically. Automatically means without conscious attention, and this is especially significant because "automaticity" is an important strategy for how humans manage their limited cognitive resources. Think about learning to drive, or learning to read. When first learning, your mind was occupied by the mechanics of what you were doing (or trying to do). You thought consciously about moving your foot from the gas pedal to the brake; you thought consciously about the sounds letters made as you worked to decode a word. There were few, if any, mental resources left over to do other things at the same time. In the case of driving, this meant that you couldn't think about what you might like to make for dinner that night (at least not without increasing your chances of having an accident). In the case of reading, it meant that by the time you had worked out the letter–sound relationships of the words in a sentence, the *meaning* (your comprehension) of the previous sentence was likely lost. Since people learn to read so that they can read to learn, they can't afford to expend valuable cognitive resources on decoding that are needed for comprehension. They need to achieve automaticity in decoding, as a foundation for comprehension. Automaticity is achieved through deliberate practice, and the amount of time spent on deliberate practice is another hallmark characteristic of experts, regardless of the arena. The challenge in the domain of inquiry is the same. It is important to intentionally cultivate and practice an *inquiry habit of mind* (Earl & Katz, 2006)—a habit of using inquiry—to engage in evidence-informed thinking about the current state, the ideal state, how to bridge the gap, and what progress is being made.

FROM RELATIONSHIPS TO DEEP COLLABORATION

Think back to the earlier discussion on Church and colleagues' (2002) network model of threads, knots, and nets. Relationships are the threads of learning networks that come together in the knots of collaboration. The knots represent the activities—the structures and content—of collaboration. Collaboration is the "work" of networks. The knots are the places where good work needs to be done if learning networks are to fulfill their efficacious ambitions. It's what most people think about as the purpose of the networks; collaboration is why you would want to bring people together. Moreover, a focus on activities helps resist privileging the threads (relationships) as ends in and of themselves. However, not all collaborations are equal, and working together for the sake of working together is not enough to move improvement forward. Collaboration is an important beginning but an insufficient end. Collaboration is a contributing ingredient in that key enabler of knowledge creation and sharing that we identified as *focused collaborative inquiry that challenges thinking and practice.* In a sense, this is a special, high-leverage form of collaboration, but groups don't get there directly. It takes time, effort, and deliberate practice, and getting there means first understanding the starting point and the envisioned end-point.

The knots of collaboration are the vehicles through which learning communities at both the school and the network levels conduct the work of improvement. In their most basic form, such vehicles include anything and everything from workshops, leadership institutes, internships, and conferences (Firestone & Pennell, 1997), through teacher research teams, study groups, and other informal groups (Lieberman & Grolnick, 1996), to the kind of cross-site teams described by Smith and Wohlstetter (2001)—management, integration, and improvement. In promise, collaborative practice can allow innovations to spread beyond single sites, build consistent modes of operation (Smith & Wohlstetter, 2001), acknowledge tough problems of teaching (Firestone & Pennell, 1997), build commitment through group understanding (Lieberman & Grolnick, 1996), and solve issues of mutual concern (Wohlstetter & Smith, 2000).

For collaboration to be an enabler of the kind of meaningful professional learning that can impact on practice, it needs to be more than just an inventory of group-based activities that we hope will make a difference. Judith Warren Little (1990) set forth the following useful fourfold taxonomy for examining collaboration as it ranges "from sporadic contacts and idiosyncratic affiliations among peers to joint work of a more rigorous and enduring sort" (p. 4). We find it to be a useful organizer for thinking about and interrogating existing practices.

1. *Storytelling and scanning for ideas:* These are occasional forays in search of specific ideas, solutions, and reassurances. Contacts are opportunistic. Teachers gain information and assurance in the quick exchange of stories. Teacher autonomy rests on freedom from scrutiny and the right to exercise personal preference. This is a conservative, individualistic culture that is very much based in the here and now, in which casual camaraderie and friendships remain at a distance from the classroom.

2. *Aid and assistance:* This describes collaborative encounters that are about the ready availability of mutual aid or helping. There is the expectation that colleagues will give one another help and/or advice when asked but not interfere in another's work in unwarranted ways. Questions asked are interpreted as requests for help. The culture of individualism, presentism, and conservatism is sustained. At issue are questions about the quality of solicited advice. There is an inherent danger, in that supplied sympathy has the potential to dissuade teachers from more analytic examinations of practice.

3. *Sharing:* This is about the routine sharing of methods and materials or the open exchange of ideas and opinions. By making these aspects of their work accessible to others, teachers expose their ideas and intentions to one another. Sharing is variable in form and consequence. It may be permissive or obligatory, may engage more or fewer teachers, may be more or less reciprocal, and so on. However, the sharing does not extend to direct commentary on curriculum, learning, and instruction.

4. *Joint work:* In Little's (1990) words, these are "encounters among teachers that rest on shared responsibility for the work of teaching (interdependence), collective conceptions of autonomy, support for teachers' initiative with regard to professional practice, and group affiliations grounded in professional work" (p. 10). Motivation to participate is grounded in needing each other's contributions in order to transcend the status quo and succeed in their own work. Members balance personal support with critical inquiry about present practice and future direction (Borko, 2004; Hudson-Ross, 2001). Scrutiny of practice within a group is

sustained where competence and commitment are not in doubt—in other words, when there is enough relational trust to support this risk taking. Moderate professional (not personal) conflict is essential for the development of high joint benefit, but the desire to avoid conflict can undermine this outcome (Engestrom, 1999).

Looking across the four forms of collaboration, it is obvious that joint work is something of a different order that includes de-privatization and a collective commitment to change. Simple intensity of collaboration cannot automatically be taken as a precursor to improvement. In fact, it is quite possible that increased contact among network members can work to perpetuate unhelpful norms if all that happens is that the cognitive biases that work to preserve and conserve our existing understandings are simply reinforced. For collaboration to enable knowledge creation and sharing, practitioners need to be able to make their knowledge accessible and explicit, and then to subject it to scrutiny and challenge in an evidence-driven sense. However, this kind of prerequisite is not always consistent with much of teachers' practical knowledge. This is why joint work that challenges thinking and practice is a relative rarity on the landscape of educational practice, though it is the critical core of the kind of collaboration that it induces changes in practice and ultimately impacts on student learning (Earl & Katz, 2006; Katz, Earl, Ben Jafaar, et al., 2008; Timperley, Wilson, Barrar, & Fung, 2008).

We believe joint work that challenges thinking and practices may be at the heart of the power of networks. Networks can provide the forum for colleagues to address genuinely new, and often difficult, ideas in a safe environment, away from the risk of retribution or censure in their daily place of work. Once the ideas are more fully developed and stabilized, these colleagues can stimulate and lead the same discussions in schools with confidence, and make the ideas practical and personal so that they are more likely to be considered for action in the school.

NLCs have the potential to support the movement toward joint work as a habit of practice. They can champion and scaffold professional learning efforts through a particular methodological engine, one that we have come to call *focused collaborative inquiry*.

GETTING TO POWERFUL COLLABORATIVE INQUIRY

In our theory of action, we noted the high-leverage potential of collaborative inquiry that challenges thinking and practice. We suggested collaborative inquiry that challenges the status quo enables the kind of professional learning that contributes to changed practice. Our research has shown, however, that collaborative inquiry is not a well-established practice in education. Because collaborative inquiry constitutes the "work" of effective learning communities in both schools and networks, it is an important new skill that requires cultivation. At the very least, it rests on a foundation of three interrelated concepts: relationships, collaboration, and inquiry. We will consider each of them separately throughout this book, but for now let's focus on inquiry.

Networks create opportunities for schools (and individuals) to learn *from* one another. The broader learning opportunity speaks to the role of inquiry in relation to establishing a needs-based focus and, as we will see later, in moving it forward. At its heart, inquiry is about a need to know, about a need for deep understanding. It is what underlies the practice of experts that we referenced earlier in terms of representing problems and challenges at a deeper level.

> *Inquiry Habit of Mind:* A mind-set of being in charge of one's own destiny, always needing to know more and creating or locating the knowledge that will be useful for reflection and for focused planning and decision making along the way.

Professional decisions in schools historically have been based on tacit knowledge, knowledge that grows out of personal beliefs and experiences. Tacit knowledge is rooted in a combination of individuals' cultural and technical histories. Cultural histories are experiences that shape cognitive patterns (or ways of thinking), while technical histories are experiences that inform what individuals come to know, the content of people's thoughts. Human beings are all predisposed to preserve existing understandings of the world and to attempt to make new things familiar by transforming them into something that is consistent with what is already known (or believed to be true). Otherwise, we would be overwhelmed by the sheer volume of novelty that would confront us around every corner. Psychologists use the term *assimilation* to describe the phenomenon by which human beings try to make new things familiar so that they fit with what we already think and believe (Piaget, 1967). But such preservation and conservation—known collectively as *cognitive biases*—make it difficult for people to engage in what psychologists call conceptual change—*real* changes in how and what people think and know that enable them to see the world differently (Katz & Earl, 2006).

Valuing deep understanding doesn't mean devaluing tacit knowledge. To embrace inquiry is not to marginalize professional judgment. Rather, inquiry provides the mechanism to facilitate the shift from what Michael Barber (2002) calls *uninformed* professional judgment to *informed* professional judgment. The practice of inquiry promotes the challenge and reconstruction of professional knowledge on the basis of a body of evidence. Intuition and gut feeling—the foundation of tacit knowledge—become hypotheses to be confirmed or challenged in relation to the available evidence. Ignoring tacit knowledge in the service of inquiry is a mistake. It is important to embrace, and even more important to explicate, tacit knowledge. Tacit knowledge provides the filter through which people interpret the evidence that is available in the service of "inquiry." Making tacit knowledge, beliefs, and assumptions explicit means declaring the nature of the filters that will influence what people look for, what they find, and how they understand it. This is why inquiry, in our view, doesn't start with data—it starts with tacit knowledge and reframing it from what is "known" to what people *think* they know." What they "think they know" then gets considered in relation to evidence and adjusted accordingly.

By recognizing the natural human propensity for assimilation, it is possible to understand just how difficult "inquiry"—as a search for deep understanding—truly is. Deep understanding very often means much more than confirming what people think they know; it means *changing* what people think and know. Inquiry involves changing the filter in a way that fits the evidence, not just engaging with the evidence in a way that fits the filter. This is the hard work of conceptual change. It means learning to live with the ambiguity and the feeling of dissonance as tacit knowledge and evidence butt heads. And, even more than this, it means recognizing that this kind of psychological discomfort is a necessary precursor to real new understanding.

> As Rita and Joan discovered, relationships in a network take time to develop. They serve as safe spaces to articulate concerns and have dialogues about what we don't know and identify what we need to find out next.
>
> Rita was sitting in her office when three teachers knocked on her office door. They wanted to talk to her about a staffroom conversation that was upsetting them. They heard that there was going to be a very strong emphasis on reading this year because the literacy results were really low and that the Grade 2 and 3 teachers were to blame for not preparing the students well. They felt that this was an unfair approach and that they were working on reading with a lot of different well-known strategies that other schools were also using. It wasn't their fault that the scores were low. These were tough kids to teach.
>
> Rita listened to the teachers and realized they were quite anxious. She asked them to take a seat and started to explain about working on a particular aspect of literacy with a network of schools experiencing the same challenges as they were. She reminded them about the time that they had spent looking at the standards-based results and told them that the other schools were now using the same process so that they could work together to learn about and target ways of really helping their students. It took a while to reassure the teachers that there was no blame being assigned and that the focus would not just be literacy, but specifically "making inferences" in reading comprehension—something that the network leadership team had only come to realize was an issue in all the schools in the network after carefully examining the results. She acknowledged that it was tough, but that they were in a network to get better results together. They agreed to discuss the detailed results again at the next staff meeting so that all staff would be on the same page.
>
> When the teachers left the office reassured, Rita felt uncertain about how she was going to move forward. She did not have the literacy expertise to guide her teachers. She was a PE teacher before becoming a principal and she did not know enough about literacy. She just did not have the capacity to be an instructional leader when it came to literacy, and it was clear that her teachers really did need that kind of support.
>
> Rita started to wonder: if this was going to be the focus, was she the best person for the job of leading the school in this direction? A little concerned with the situation, she wanted to talk to someone who would understand her concern. Remembering Joan's comments on not being an expert, she decided to call Joan.

Joan's phone rang just after she had finished disciplining two students for bullying. She felt very frustrated and tired. When Joan answered the phone, Rita was on the other end and there was anxiety in her voice.

Joan: Rita, are you okay?

Rita: Well, yes . . . no. I am not sure about this network thing. I feel out of my depth.

Joan: What are you talking about? You have been a principal for six years now.

Rita: Yes, but I am not talking about that. I am talking about the fact that I don't know much about reading strategies and I know almost nothing about teaching kids to make inferences. I had to look it up and ask my teachers about it. And they are going to be looking to me for instructional leadership. Maybe I should be a part of a network that has a focus on something that I know more about.

Joan: I don't think so. Although that would feel comfortable, it wouldn't really be about a "learning" network then. We're in this because of what we need to learn, not what we already know.

Joan and Rita talked for a while. Joan had a limited background in literacy and Rita had none. As they talked through the issue of leading this kind of focus, they recognized that the rest of their principal colleagues in the network probably had similar backgrounds. They decided that it would be important to investigate this issue with the network group because it had to do with capacity and roles in the network. They thought it would be important to talk through the issue of roles because, even if there was a principal with a literacy background, the administrative duties in any school would not afford them the time to directly support their teachers.

When Joan hung up the phone, she felt a degree of stress and renewed energy at the same time. She had helped a colleague in her network because she was trusted. It felt good to be part of something that was bigger than discipline and management in her school. She looked forward to the conversation with the network because she felt a sense of complete ambiguity on how they were going to use the network to promote student reading comprehension learning.

Time for Reflection

To what extent is there relational trust in your school?

List all of the collaborative activities in which you are currently involved in the school. Locate each of them in relation to Little's (1990) categories—story swapping, aid and assistance, sharing, and joint work.

What could you do to cultivate trust in your school?

5

Leadership in Networked Professional Learning Communities

In our theory of action, we explained that both informal and formal leadership are important ingredients in instructional leadership, that important key enabler of professional knowledge creation. Leadership, defined by activity rather than formal position, unfolds both within schools and between the schools that together comprise the network. In this chapter, we begin with the role of formal leaders in networked learning communities (NLCs) and then examine how informal leadership works.

ROLES OF FORMAL LEADERS

Formal leadership is critical in the work of NLCs—at both the school and network levels. We certainly know a great deal about the importance of administrators in the work of schools and student achievement (Robinson, 2007). We won't go into detail here because this is not a book about leadership. Rather, we are concerned with the importance of formal leadership in networks, and how that leadership crosses the boundaries between schools and within schools, because, as we've said before, schools are the locus of change in thinking and practice.

Formal leadership in NLCs matters from the very beginning. It is the administrators (both school and district leaders) who together provide the formal leadership of the network and are the architects and pioneers of this intentional organizational form for school improvement. When the Networked Learning Group in England built that country's Networked Learning Communities Program, it made formal co-leadership a requirement for school networks. Co-leaders not only handle the logistical things like arranging refreshments and booking meeting rooms, but also take responsibility for consulting with the others in order to build the agenda, chairing the meetings, and representing the network in broader district conversations. They are the interface or the boundary spanners between the network and beyond. For example, when the group decides to solicit the advice or support of a particular curriculum specialist, it is a network co-leader who extends the invitation.

You might wonder about the rationale for having two leaders (co-leaders), but we have found it to be beneficial in a climate of personnel transience. Remember that network membership is defined not by the person but by the school. The needs-based school focus, the glue that binds schools in a network together, determines network membership. When an administrator moves to a new school, his or her previous school stays in the network but the individual might not (depending on the new assignment). Co-leadership provides leadership stability so that transfers allow continuity and succession planning. A new co-leader can be mentored into the role by a continuing co-leader.

Our research on leadership in networks has found that formal leaders play a critical role in what we might call "enabling activities" (Earl & Katz, 2007). We have found that the involvement of formal leaders in such enabling activities is correlated with changes in thinking and practice at both the school and network levels. Formal school leaders are positioned as boundary spanners and facilitators of change because they are situated both in the school and in the network. They provide both a point of upload and download of ideas and practices between the school and the network, and they facilitate the conditions for other boundary spanners to emerge from within the school. They also help foster a school culture that contributes to the way school colleagues relate to one another and to the network in order to leverage changes in thinking and practice.

Moving beyond network co-leadership, our work (Earl and Katz, 2007) has revealed four important roles that formal leaders (whether school or district) play in relation to networks:

1. Encouraging and motivating others

2. Setting and monitoring the agenda

3. Sharing leadership

4. Building capacity and providing support

Encouraging and Motivating Others

Network involvement prompts formal leaders to identify others in their schools and encourage them to get involved. Often this means creating motivation among members of staff and inspiring them to play a role. It entails cultivating a climate of intellectual challenge in schools because engagement with the network should enable the conditions for new professional learning in a focus area. It is about instilling a sense of "urgency" for the new learning—new learning for teachers, that is—that responds to a school-based student learning need, and enabling the "agency" to identify, develop, and execute the requisite job-embedded learning program.

Educators are often confronted with the quintessential challenge that Plato identified and set out in his famous paradox: we don't know what we don't know. And yet, to engage in new learning, they need to know that they don't know. The Greek word *aporia* captures this concept. Loosely translated, it describes the necessary state of awareness in which you know that you don't know and need to learn something new. Conscious and explicit "not knowing" is not easy, given the human psychological predispositions to stability. If "not knowing" is a perceived sign of professional weakness that prompts a fear of exposure, it becomes even more difficult. There is a strange irony in that, although education is a learning profession, teachers are not always quick to admit to "not knowing" in any kind of public or semipublic arena, especially in areas that they believe they should already "know" about. An important part of the encouragement and motivation role that formal leaders play, then, is to model what "not knowing" looks like in authentic ways, using themselves as examples. When leaders provide these models, it has the potential to create a learning spiral, with leader learning enabling teacher learning, which in turn enables student learning.

Much of the leader learning that the network can support is related to enabling processes. Leaders don't have an impact on classroom practice directly. They cultivate the conditions for the kind of job-embedded teacher professional learning that will influence classroom practice. The question of *how* to cultivate the conditions for this kind of professional learning in the focus area defines the collaborative learning for leaders in the network. But questions of *how*—like creating conditions for school-level implementation, for example—can't typically be considered detached from the *what*—the content of the focus. Such content learning—also a necessity for formal leaders—offers a good opportunity for leaders to encourage and motivate through modeling. For many formal leaders, this means new content learning themselves. In our literacy example, for instance, it is certainly reasonable to assume that not all principals or district leaders are literacy experts to the point of understanding what it takes to analyze student work to understand reading comprehension needs. People come to formal leadership positions from various histories and trajectories. Leading learning and practicing instructional leadership in response to a needs-based focus likely require some new content learning for administrators, in addition to the "process" work.

In much the same way as we are describing here, Stein and Nelson (2003) have observed that, as administrator levels increase and functions become broader, leadership content knowledge becomes less fine grained. They suggest that administrators need solid mastery of at least one subject, including the learning and teaching of it (so that they understand what it means to really know something), and that they develop expertise in other subjects by what they call "postholing"—the in-depth explorations of an important but bounded slice of the subject, how it is learned, and how it is taught. The needs-based focus of the network provides just such a bounded slice for leaders to model learning and inquiry, and to encourage and motivate others to learn as well.

Setting and Monitoring the Agenda

Formal leaders are responsible for setting the vision and priorities, and for ensuring that the work of the network and the schools is purposeful and focused. In other words, these leaders need to work to make sure that the network purpose is paramount, and that the needs-based learning focus is privileged in the school's improvement work. In our earlier description of *initiativitis*—the disease of the initiative—we talked about how important focus is as a mechanism for aiming improvement activity. The network focus needs to be right, shared, and understood, both across and within schools. Schools in a given network are there because of a shared school-based focus—that is, the network and school foci must be aligned. And because the school is the locus of change in thinking and practice, the focus needs to instill a sense of urgency, unite the improvement activities of the school, and orient them in a particular direction. That's why it has to be needs based.

We are often asked how it is that a school can have a single focus. We are challenged to "get real" because schools are complex places with multiple needs. We are given evidence to support this argument in the form of school improvement plans that require the specification of multiple goals (for some reason, three seems to be the magic number!) and we are told the degrees of freedom for these school plans are delimited by the overarching district improvement plan. We don't take issue with any of this. But we do maintain that when schools attempt to cover the range of possibilities and actualities, their improvement efforts are "a mile wide and an inch deep." Scarcity is the foundational concept of economics and, to the extent that resources (defined in whatever way you like) are limited, schools need to be purposeful and intentional in deciding where to orient their efforts. And they need to keep their effort focused until they have evidence suggesting they have accomplished their goal and it is time to move on. The prevailing mile-wide mentality has the effect of turning practitioners into improvement bumblebees, flitting from one thing to the next. Our push for focus is the equivalent of the "postholing" that Stein and Nelson (2003) describe. Of course, there are multiple needs. But to really make a difference in any of them requires using evidence to identify the most urgent, channel the resources and efforts, and stay the course.

When we say that formal leaders are responsible for setting and monitoring the agenda, we mean that they lead in the identifying, directing, and sustaining that goes into establishing and maintaining the focus. We have already described what leading the establishment of focus looks like, but once there is an agreed-upon focus, the challenge is to stick with it. Leaders support staying the course in two ways—alignment and buffering. Alignment means helping maintain the network focus in schools by showing staff how it fits with other pieces, most often other district requirements. Connecting the dots in this way shouldn't be forced. The staff need to see the professional learning focus as an initiative that does not compete with others. And when schools feel bombarded by multiple requirements that are indeed quite disparate, with the potential to detract from the network focus as people assume a reactive posture, responding to whatever it is that comes down the pipe, formal leaders play the critical role of buffering—protecting the focus in the network and the schools from competing influences that, though likely important, can become activity traps. This is particularly important when the learning demands of the network focus intensify, and it may be easier to move to something new than to really change existing practices. Unlike alignment, the buffering role is one practiced by effective network leaders but not always discussed explicitly because protecting the network focus can be construed as noncompliance. Even though people readily admit that you can't do everything that you're asked to do, they are not as willing to accept that you don't do everything. Formal leaders protect the needs-based focus by helping (or giving permission to!) those around them to prioritize, and, in the words of a leader we know, to decide "what gets a nod and wink" and what gets real, focused, ongoing attention.

As the network meeting was about to start, a buzz of conversations filled the room. The principals were talking about their excitement and frustrations in trying to fulfill their formal leadership role in schools by promoting the network focus while grappling with all the mandated initiatives from the district.

The school leaders were all chatting to one another about how they used the literacy results in their schools to promote the focus. Rita was telling Elsie about a great session that she had at her all-school staff meeting where she presented the findings of the students achievement data and the teachers worked together to share their current practices; Charles was talking about a meeting that he had with his Grade 3–5 teachers to look over the achievement data and talk through the issues around reading comprehension; and Rikard was describing a problem with getting some of his teachers to accept the network focus. Joan started the meeting with an invitation to the principals to offer a three-minute update on the situation in their schools. She wanted to create a routine-sharing protocol in the meetings to make sure that all the members in the group were always aware of each other's important issues and successes.

As the individuals told their brief school stories, the conversation converged on Rikard's issue.

Rikard: It was my vice principal who was dealing with the criticism from teachers. Apparently, since the staff meeting where we presented the results and the focus, teachers have been approaching my VP telling her that it is all too much. There are two district initiatives already being promoted, one on "evidence-informed decision making" and the other on "case management." The teachers are feeling pulled in three directions and they are stressed about it.

Joan: My teachers did mention that the district PD that is being offered is not about literacy strategies. But, apart from that, they have been very good about the focus. But for us, it is not new. We are just narrowing our attention from "literacy" to "inference in reading comprehension."

Rita: There are always a number of initiatives going on at once. I have never taught in a school where you don't feel pulled in a number of directions.

Charles: I agree with you. But isn't that the point of this focus—to try to focus on one thing and do it really well rather than doing everything without doing anything really well?

Joan: Yes.

Elsie: The memo that came from the district about the case management—that was about at-risk students, right?

Rikard: Yes, it is about identifying and tracking at-risk kids so that their written response work could be analyzed, and targeted instructional strategies could be implemented.

Elsie: And the evidence-informed mandate from the district was about using data to make decisions, right?

Rikard: Yes, that is right.

Elsie: Well, I really don't see any problem. There is no conflict. The teachers just don't see it because they are thinking in compartments rather than holistically.

Joan: What do you mean?

Elsie: Well, like we discussed last time, I did go through the reading comprehension data analysis protocol with my leadership team. We got the same results as everyone here. We have a serious problem with inference and making connections. But when we went over the detailed results, we noticed that most of the questions in these two categories required written responses. So we gathered samples of written responses from our students at risk and had a good look at them. We are starting to really see where we need to make some instructional changes.

Joan: I'd love to see what you have done—maybe at our next meeting. It sounds interesting, and by doing this you are also respecting the district mandates.

Elsie: Yes, but I did not purposefully set out to do that. I was working with the guidelines that we agreed on in our network. The rest just fell into place. That is my point!

Rikard: Hmm. That does make sense. The district mandates support the work that we are already doing.

Charles: I think that the big difference with us is that we are saying that we are following the district mandates—but we are limiting the scope to making inferences in reading comprehension because that is our network focus.

Joan: It does make the work more manageable.

Charles: Yes, it does. But it also means two things. One, we should be working with a case-management strategy within the network. It shouldn't be hard since we are already working from data. We just need to pay particular attention to the students who are at risk, like Elsie has. And two, we need a good communication strategy with our teachers so that they know that the network focus is the priority.

Joan: I agree. We can worry about the district alignment piece. And they can worry about improving inference skills in their students.

Rikard: I never thought of that in explicit terms. But it is about job-embedded strategies within our focus. This will definitely help at my school.

Joan: I think that we have all benefited from this conversation. And so will our teachers!

Sharing Leadership

Formal leaders in networks work to intentionally broaden the base of leadership to include informal or distributed leadership, the kind of leadership that is located in teaching and learning and determined by expertise. People are the medium through which networks do their work. Formal leaders look to "experts" to lead the work of professional learning within the network. Sometimes the expertise is located outside of the network, but often the capacity resides within the network. The goal of formal leaders is to locate and unleash the expertise and create the conditions for "lateral" capacity building across the network. Effective formal leaders in networks share leadership by enabling others in the school to become informal leaders in the school and in the network. In networks that we've studied

(Earl & Katz, 2007), formal leaders describe themselves as gatekeepers of leadership. These formal leaders recognize that a key dimension of their own learning needs is to learn how to create the conditions for empowerment of others as a strategy for moving the learning focus forward across all of their schools. Formal leaders acknowledge their reliance on the expertise, abilities, qualities, and talents of other individuals, and are aware of a need to defer to this expertise and to not interfere with it. Leadership emerges from a number of people in a wide range of configurations. Sometimes these roles are directly in the network, while at other times they are localized within the school but connected to activities that relate to the network focus.

Building Capacity and Providing Support

The network focus defines an urgent area of professional learning need, and ultimately what formal leaders do and need to do is work to intentionally facilitate capacity building. We are talking about building capacity in the key enablers of professional knowledge creation—the processes and practices that make schools innovative knowledge communities—as well as capacity in the network learning focus. Mitchell and Sackney (2001) describe three mutually influencing and interdependent categories of capacity that formal leaders can facilitate:

1. Personal capacity—the active and reflective construction of knowledge

2. Interpersonal capacity—collegial relations and collective practice

3. Organizational capacity—building structures that create and maintain sustainable organizational processes

In their view, these categories form the curriculum for building professional capacity in professional learning communities. At the personal level, individuals are learning pragmatic skills and knowledge and extending their personal coping and problem-solving abilities. At the interpersonal level, the network members are learning how to interact, cooperate, and share information with one another. At the organizational level, they are learning about how to construct and adapt the organization for the mutual benefit of all the members. These categories are not mutually exclusive, and they are often nested within each other in complex ways. What's important from our point of view is the recognition that formal leaders can intentionally construct their roles so as to move each of these forward, a task best accomplished not in a vacuum, but embedded within the substance that is given by the network focus.

ROLES OF INFORMAL LEADERS

While formal leadership is defined by role and position, informal leadership is activity based and thus broadens the conception of what counts as leadership in important ways. Spillane (2006) makes the case that leadership in schools (and, we would add, networks) is not connected to role or position but to activities and practices that are stretched over many people in a system of interactions. This portrayal of leadership allows many people to perform leadership work to influence the core of schooling: curriculum, teaching, and learning. And this is the crux of the contribution informal leadership makes as a key building block of capacity in focused *instructional* leadership—that critical enabler of focused professional learning. To the extent that informal leadership is defined as such, because the relevant leadership practices are inscribed in activity and expertise that is based in content competencies, both the "focused" and the "instructional" dimensions of the requisite capacity are underscored.

The next meeting demonstrated that, as formal leaders, the principals had collaborated to construct a focused network. The next step was to create conditions for informal leadership in the network.

As Joan sat in the meeting, she recognized that a real sense of trust and excitement had formed in the group. They were not just exchanging stories or talking about superficial school issues, they were focused on exchanging ideas about what they were doing in their schools and figuring out how to make things work together. This was the depth of conversation she had sought, but they had not really reached the point that addressed the reason for her first call to Carl—moving her "stuck" school forward. As a team, they had identified the area of student learning that was shared as an issue amongst the schools—making inferences in reading comprehension. But they still did not have an effective solution. She thought about the conversation she had with Rita and realized that this was the moment that she needed to share their concerns with the group.

Joan: I think that we are at the point where we really need to consider a joint strategy for the focus now. We have been talking about how to lead the focus as principals. Now that we are on the same page with that, we need to move into changing the literacy strategies being used in our classrooms. I have heard several suggestions that sound reasonable, but sounding reasonable is not good enough. The initiatives that I supported over the last three years all sounded reasonable, but my student literacy scores did not improve! I don't want to continue investing time and money and not making a difference that has results.

Rikard: I agree—it is frustrating. We don't have a shortage of strategy ideas.

Elsie: Maybe we need to find out about the strategies we are already using in our schools and put them beside our student achievement data to see whether we can identify two or three that are most effective. We can all agree to use those and then monitor the improvement in literacy scores by strategy. This way, we can make an evidence-informed decision about next steps.

Rikard: I like the idea of continuing to use data to check for our progress.

Rita: I do too, but honestly I am no literacy expert and I think that we need to move beyond our group for expertise. I don't know what I need to do to target "making inferences" for the students and I don't know if the teachers do either. I don't know how to support my teachers as an instructional leader. I have a literacy lead in my school who is more of an expert in that area. I count on her for this kind of thing.

Elsie: I count on my literacy lead too, but from the analysis of results it sounds like our literacy leads need some help, too.

Rikard: My literacy lead and some of my teachers have taken a few professional development workshops on specific literacy strategies. And I am not seeing the results that I want in my school either. But I do think that they are trying their best. I don't know if it is the strategies, the implementation, or too many directions.

Carl: It seems to me that we have defined the student learning need, and now we are talking about defining the matching teacher learning need. What do you think?

Elsie: That is exactly where I am at. But I have to agree with Rikard that I don't really know what teachers need to know in relation to reading comprehension and making inferences. I can't be an expert at it—I am too busy running the school.

Joan: We can't possibly lead in all areas with the level of expertise that is required. Like you said, I am also too busy running the school. But I do think that it is up to us to offer the support mechanisms for the teachers to be able to have that type of leadership.

Rita: So we agree that we don't need to know about literacy!

Carl: I don't know if that would be a fair statement. I think that all of you, as the formal leaders, need to lean on the local expertise in your schools. But we also need to know enough about making inferences and reading comprehension so that we can support the teachers in the school.

Charles: It seems to me that this is a good place to tap into the informal leaders in our schools. Most of us have a literacy lead in our school. If we don't, we need to appoint one. There was a district mandate last year that each school would have a literacy lead but there was little direction or guidance about their role and responsibilities.

Rita: Well, mine just left on maternity leave. I will be happy to appoint a replacement. But I could do a much better job on that if I knew what the new lead was going to do and what I am going to do.

Joan: It sounds like we need some role definitions in the network.

Rita: Maybe nothing prescriptive or too formal—just some guidelines to help.

What Is Informal Leadership?

Although our own work (Earl & Katz, 2007) has found that teachers and other staff members in NLCs are often reluctant to describe aspects of their work as "leadership"—preferring instead to reserve the term for the more formal role definition or the presence of certain personality characteristics—many of their practices reflect an influence that suggests otherwise. Building on York-Barr and Duke's (2004) definition, what constitutes informal leadership is the process by which teachers (and other staff members), individually or collectively, influence their colleagues, principals, and other members of network and school communities to improve teaching and learning practices with the aim of increased student learning and achievement.

While formal leadership is often about operational leadership and sometimes about instructional leadership, informal leadership is almost always about instructional leadership. Sherrill (1999) defined a set of core competencies that would apply to such leaders, and these included such things as demonstrating exemplary teaching and learning, understanding and sharing relevant theory and research, and guiding colleagues by means of reflection and an inquiry orientation. When it comes to instructional leadership, research finds that this kind of work is in fact done more often by others in the school than by principals (Spillane, Camburn, & Pareja, 2007).

The work that has been done on informal leadership points to a range of instructional leadership-type activities in which these people might engage. In their review of the relevant research, York-Barr and Duke (2004) concluded that informal leadership includes a wide variety of work at multiple levels in educational systems, including work with students, colleagues, and formal administrators. Our own research on informal leadership in NLCs (Earl & Katz, 2007) identified the kinds of activities at both the school and network levels that Katzenmeyer and Moller (2001) describe as leading within and beyond the classroom, contributing to a community of teachers, learners, and leaders, and influencing others toward improved educational practice. Informal leaders were involved in coordinating activities in the school and network; establishing action plans; providing support, resources, and information to colleagues; evaluating progress; and encouraging others to seek advice.

As we've said time and again, focus is foremost when it comes to both within- and across-school learning communities being impactful. As such, informal leadership is often embodied in activities that are imbued with a content expertise that is related to the focus or, more specifically, to focused professional learning. Non-administrator leaders in networks do things like lead training sessions and participate in collaborative groups designed to deepen professional knowledge and to share learning in specific domains that are relevant to the school and network foci. It is interesting to us that the teachers and other staff members who we've observed taking leadership roles talk predominantly about what they are doing in working with their colleagues and sharing their knowledge. Their roles as leaders are most often a function of their relationships, influence, and activities, not roles where they have power over their colleagues, except by persuasion.

The Interdependence of Informal and Formal Leadership

In many ways, informal leadership as a key dimension or constituent of building capacity in focused instructional leadership is best illustrated in relation to its formal leadership counterpart. The roles of informal leaders in learning communities–although multiple and varied—are often defined and conceptualized in ways that are connected to what formal leaders do. Leithwood and colleagues (2007) looked at various leadership functions in this way and found the following:

- With respect to setting direction, informal leaders had more involvement with creating high-performance expectations and motivating others than formal leaders, while formal leaders had more to do with identifying and articulating a vision.
- In relation to developing people, non-administrator leaders were more focused on providing individual support and modeling appropriate values and practices than formal leaders.
- Informal leaders were more involved with executing organizational design than formal leaders. Of particular importance (for our focus on learning networks) were the functions of building collaborative processes and building community.
- Non-administrator leaders devoted more of their attention to managing programs, committees, and meetings and sharing information than formal leaders, while administrators more often took care of delegating.

There is an interdependence between what formal and informal leaders do such that formal leaders enable informal leaders to lead in ways that are activity based and expertise driven. Formal leaders *distribute* power and leadership so as to encourage others to view themselves as important in shaping future direction. And, of course, it is formal leaders who officially sanction school participation in NLCs.

At the next meeting, the group of principals worked to define their roles and the roles of the literacy leads with respect to the learning expectations in the network.

Carl led them through the exercise in the following box. First, they delineated what they thought the teacher learning needs might be, based on the student learning need. Second, after some discussion, they decided that those learning needs would be the foundation of their expectations in terms of what the teachers would learn and do in the schools. Third, they considered what level of expertise and leadership they expected from literacy leads in the schools. Finally, they considered their own roles and responsibilities in relation to the current roles of the literacy leads.

Teacher Learning Focus	
Strategies for making inferences in reading comprehension	• Understanding and recognizing learning outcomes related to making inferences • Recognizing different levels of making inferences in student work • Knowledge of instructional strategies to promote skills in making inferences • Creating targeted learning opportunities for students to make and practice making inferences in class • Assessing teaching strategies and student work for improvement in making inferences • Collaborating with teachers in the school and in the network to enhance their capacity for teaching students to make inferences

From Expectations of Teacher Learning to Actions		
Expectations: Teachers will...	Literacy leaders need to directly support...	School leaders need to...
Understand and recognize learning outcomes for making inferences	Knowledge of learning outcomes for making inferences Recognize learning outcomes related to making inferences at each grade level	Be able to define and recognize making inferences in reading comprehension
Recognize different levels of responses in student work for making inferences	Knowledge of skill levels for making inferences Identification of skill levels from student work	Support literacy leads in becoming local literacy experts Support teachers to learn, practice, and reflect on the implementation Provide teachers with time and resources for learning
Know the instructional strategies that promote skills to make inferences	Knowledge of relevant instructional strategies	
Create learning opportunities in their classes that target the particular learning needs of their students	Skills in implementing strategies as needed	

(Continued)

(Continued)

From Expectations of Teacher Learning to Actions		
Expectations: Teachers will . . .	Literacy leaders need to directly support . . .	School leaders need to . . .
Assess their teaching strategies and student work for improvement in making inferences	Monitoring and assessing changes in teaching strategies Monitoring and assessing student work	
Collaborate with their colleagues in the network and school to enhance everyone's knowledge and skills	Systematically sharing resources, strategies, and learning with colleagues Developing local approaches with colleagues	Create conditions for teachers to collaborate

The leadership team members reviewed the chart, and it quickly became clear that they would be relying on their literacy leads as experts to directly support the teachers' learning about the most appropriate and effective literacy strategies based on the students' learning needs. Their role as the formal leaders would be to offer the organizational support to achieve the expectations.

The principals agreed that they needed to talk to their literacy leads as soon as possible in order to proceed. Their plan would be useless unless the literacy leads agreed. The literacy leads might also have some different ideas about the learning that was required, since that was their area of expertise.

Each principal would return to his or her school and talk to the literacy lead about (i) the school focus, (ii) the evolving network, (iii) beginning ideas about the learning he or she needed to support, and, most importantly, (iv) a mechanism for bringing the literacy leads into the process to push the focus forward.

In two weeks, the principals would meet to share their impressions and the information they gathered from the leads so they could make a responsive procedural plan.

Time for Reflection

Describe an occasion when a formal leader created the conditions for staff to focus on improving their work.

How do new ideas come into your school?

Who are the informal leaders in your school? Describe how they are leaders and what gives them influence.

6

From Student Learning to Teacher Learning

Thus far, we've talked about focus in terms of student learning and how aiming improvement is most efficient when it is driven by a consideration of student learning needs. In the closing section of the previous chapter, we looked at the relationship between formal and informal leadership whereby the former begins to cultivate the conditions for the latter by realizing that student learning needs and teacher learning needs are interrelated. We unpack this important relationship in more detail here.

Having a clear, visible, and shared focus in schools and networks is an important feature of networked learning communities (NLCs) designed to build and mobilize knowledge in order to improve classroom practice and increase student learning. The focus is important for bringing people together to reflect on and rethink their beliefs and their practices, and to minimize the clutter of activity. When the focus is vague or not visible, everyone might agree to it but no one feels compelled to use it to change their thinking or their practices. So the focus needs to be clear and visible to define the space for the consideration and cultivation of new learning and changed practice for teachers. Focus links student and teacher learning needs. Practitioners are generally quite comfortable and confident stating what it is that children need to learn. At the system level, a great deal of effort (broadly defined) is put into the determination of student learning needs through assessment systems that give us more and more student achievement data. This is a good thing, but it is also premised on a shaky logic model, one that suggests that the problem is primarily an identification one—that if teachers just knew what students needed to learn they would teach it. But, time and again, the research (Katz & Earl, 2005) points out that all too often the stumbling block is not identification; it is the absence of alternative ways of engaging students and of teaching the concepts— "So what do I do?" A teacher we know once summed it up succinctly when she said, "I know how to teach fractions, I just don't know what to do when they don't get it."

Student learning needs are not just student learning needs. They are also a signal for teacher learning needs. Teachers don't impact on student achievement directly. They impact on student achievement through what they do and say. When students aren't getting it (whatever "it" happens to be), it is an indication that something needs to change in teaching practice. And changing teacher practice often means new learning for teachers. NLCs exist to identify, create, support, and sustain this new professional learning. The focus of a school and of a network needs to include both student and teacher dimensions. The network does its work from a mandate that asks the critical capacity-building question: What is the necessary teacher learning that will shape practice in a way that will enable the identified student learning, and how can the network mobilize the resources and expertise to facilitate this learning?

When the focus specifies the connection between student and teacher learning needs, it provides a space to draw on new explicit knowledge and research as well as expose the tacit knowledge of the group for deeper consideration. The National College for School Leadership's Networked Learning Group talks about a model of professional learning that can be represented as three fields of knowledge (Jackson & Temperley, 2006). Figure 6.1 depicts this model. The first field is *what is known* from theory, research, and best practice. The second field is *what the group knows*, the tacit knowledge of those involved. The third field is *new knowledge* that is created together through collaborative work. Networks support knowledge creation and sharing when people from different schools in a network come together to engage in purposeful activity that considers their own know-how in relation to the public knowledge base in order to co-construct new learning.

Figure 6.1   Three Fields of Knowledge

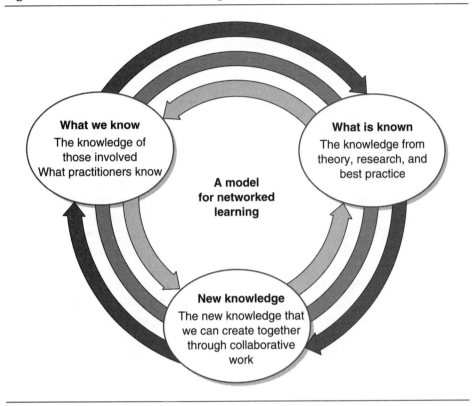

Source: Jackson & Temperley (2006).

When it comes to practitioners identifying their own learning needs in order to shift practice, they are confronted with the challenge that we referred to earlier; namely, we don't know what we don't know. And yet, if they are to engage in new learning, they need to know that they don't know. The task is to leverage the power of the network to know what the teachers collectively don't know, as a starting point for new learning.

At the next meeting, the principals decided it was time to take action to operationalize the roles they had defined to meet the network focus expectations. As the principals shared their school findings, they identified a critical need for professional learning among the literacy leads.

The principals were surprised that most of the literacy leads were working in isolation, that they didn't feel like they were valued in the school or that they weren't really welcome in classrooms, and that each one had their own focus and approach to working with their colleague and students in the school. Although the literacy leads had all been to a minimum of two workshops in the last year, the topics were varied. The literacy leads tended to promote whatever strategy they believed to be effective, but there was no direct evidence that supported the use of any chosen strategy. In fact, the only thing of which the principals were certain was that the selected strategies did not successfully target making inferences in reading comprehension. In addition, the literacy leads only received training in literacy, and not in leadership or change management.

After some discussion, the principals decided that the literacy leads needed support from the principals and from each other. The leadership group decided that the literacy leads should work in a parallel arrangement to the one for the principals in the network. The leads would meet periodically to learn about and share strategies that improved making inferences, and to learn how to successfully lead their colleagues in changing their literacy classroom practices. There was substantial discussion about how the leadership group should bring the literacy leads together. The group concluded the discussion with two decisions: first, it decided to safeguard regular contact time with classroom teachers for the literacy leads within the school day; second, it decided that an external literacy expert would be brought in to support capacity building for the literacy leads.

The principals decided that they would invite Sheryl, a well-respected literacy expert from the district office, to support the literacy lead group. Elsie knew Sheryl well and attested to the fact that Sheryl would welcome the opportunity to redirect her efforts since she did not appreciate the way in which she was currently working. Currently, Sheryl waited at the district office until a school requested her help with a specific literacy lesson. Sheryl would then model a lesson in that school and debrief it with the teachers who were willing to talk through the teaching issues. After two years of this kind of work, Sheryl had articulated her conclusion that the approach was limited in its large-scale effect.

The meeting concluded with the following action points: (1) Joan, as a network leader, would contact Sheryl to officially invite her to join the network team. (2) Each principal would talk with their literacy lead to explain the purpose of the network group and discuss how they would be supporting the focus. (3) Joan would facilitate the first literacy lead meeting to help them set up the network group.

TOWARDS FOCUSED COLLABORATIVE INQUIRY

Story swapping is nice. It responds to the need of human beings for social contact, it can be cathartic, and it can contribute to relationship building. But it can also work to protect the status quo by preserving and conserving biases, a deeply rooted propensity of people to grab hold of things that confirm their existing understandings while ignoring or dismissing those ideas that are challenging or contradictory. Learning to embrace challenge as a necessary—indeed, required—precursor of knowledge building is an important new skill and not one that people typically come to without purposeful effort. Moreover, it is not a skill that people are likely to arrive at alone. They need others to help them get there. This kind of challenging learning happens best in a collaborative environment. And it also needs to move beyond story swapping.

Our work (Katz, Earl, Ben Jafaar, et al., 2008) has identified focused collaborative inquiry as a new but powerful skill for educators. This concept merges deep collaboration in the form of rigorous and challenging joint work with inquiry, and is consistent with Little's (2005) reference to a large body of research suggesting that conditions for improving learning and teaching are strengthened when teachers collectively question ineffective teaching routines, examine new conceptions of teaching and learning, find generative means to acknowledge and respond to difference and conflict, and engage actively in supporting one another's professional growth. In our view, collaborative inquiry—especially when it is focused—is likely to be a high leverage practice, but it involves a set of skills and dispositions that are new to many schools. Participants in NLCs need to use the network to acquire this critical new set of skills in order to work together on serious issues that require investigation, reflection, and challenging of ideas.

Joan and Charles wanted to make sure the literacy leads network started on a professional learning inquiry cycle. They constructed the agenda of the first meeting to start engaging the literacy leads in question-driven inquiry.

Joan and Charles facilitated the first meeting of the literacy leads. They were aware that this group of teachers did not all know one another, and they wanted to help them start to build the professional trust required for collaborative learning. Joan started with a quick introduction of the network and how it came to be, and then presented an overview of the process that the leadership team used to systematically look over the literacy assessment results in search of a specific focus.

Joan: All of the principals in our schools have committed to supporting literacy improvement. One school in our region needed a very different focus, so that school has joined another network. Now we are ready to get going, but it was really clear that we aren't the school literacy experts—you are. We wanted to be here at the first meeting of the network of literacy leads that parallels our network of principals. The purpose is to work together toward meeting the expectations of our shared focus. We think it is a great opportunity for you to learn from one another, and have access to targeted professional development and to a literacy expert. Also, you will learn more about change-management processes.

Charles highlighted the fact that this network was different from the ones they had seen in the district because this one grew out of a shared need that came out of examining the results. He made sure the literacy leads understood that everything that had happened to date in the network development was about needs-based learning. And he made sure that they realized they were recruited to this leadership role because their principal believed that they could understand and be part of a cycle of professional inquiry in this work. Charles then asked the leads to go through the summary evidence that the principals had developed in their schools. He provided a summary of the evidence for each of the schools to all the literacy leads. The leads worked in pairs to examine the summaries of the school-level results for all the schools in the network. Their task was to identify the area they thought needed serious attention. The group reviewed the documents and had a whole-group discussion of their observations. They concluded that making inferences and connections was a weak area for students across all the schools.

At that stage, the literacy leads spent some time planning how they would work together. By the end of the meeting, they had decided they would act as a think tank where they would come up with literacy solutions for their schools, implement them, and share their progress with one another. They decided to set up an e-mail conversation with all of the literacy leads in it to carry on with the discussion. And they would have a rotating facilitator and secretary to coordinate their meetings. There were some concerns about protecting their colleagues, and they agreed that all conversations about teaching practices they observed in schools would be confidential. They also decided that they would only consider themselves successful if all of the schools improved. They agreed to take the evidence Charles gave them for each school and collate it to one network file. This file would hold the baseline evidence for their network. They decided that their first task would be to investigate the strategies that were being used to teach students to make inferences in schools. That would be the starting point for discussion at the next meeting.

Charles debriefed their plan and added his own challenge to the group: that the "literacy solutions" they ultimately developed needed to be ones that could cross over into all schools, and that these should be strategies, programs, or approaches that had been shown to work.

Charles: I think we need to take the time and do our homework up front to make sure we are selecting appropriate solutions that have strong research support. We don't want hit-and-miss solutions.

The leadership network had already figured out how to make sure that the literacy leads had the time and resources to (1) learn about effective literacy strategies and (2) learn about change-management strategies.

Joan closed the meeting by telling them that the leadership network had already begun its work by arranging for Sheryl, the district literacy expert, to work with the literacy leads as a critical friend to provide support and expertise as they worked.

The group was excited; many of them had worked with Sheryl already and they had a lot of respect for her. They thanked Joan and Charles, and a number of them stayed behind to talk about what this would mean in their work. Mat and Rochelle were responsible for the next meeting. Mat agreed he would contact Sheryl. Rochelle would sort out the e-mail process.

At the heart of focused collaborative inquiry is the recognition that it is a *methodology* for the necessary professional learning in the focus area. Collaborative inquiry is not the "it"; it is a tool in the service of the "it." The "it" is the professional learning that will move the focus forward by building the kind of knowledge that will change classroom practice in a way that responds to the student learning need. Helen Timperley and her colleagues in New Zealand (Timperley et al., 2008) have recently completed a Best Evidence Synthesis of studies in professional learning that have demonstrated impact on student learning. They have captured the inquiry process for focused professional learning in a diagram, shown in Figure 6.2.

This cycle begins with a consideration of student learning needs, moves to an explicit articulation of the relationship between teacher practice and student learning in relation to student learning requirements, and charts a course for professional learning that will deepen professional knowledge and translate into changed practice. The process is cyclical but forward moving, with explicit attention to the new practices and a return to the next consideration of student learning needs. Inquiry and professional learning are inseparable in this model; they merge in a forward-moving, *progressive* way.

Figure 6.2   Professional Learning Inquiry Cycle

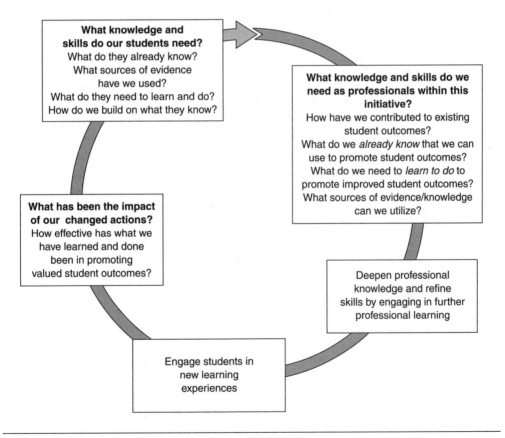

Source: Timperley et al. (2008).

When teachers engage in this kind of progressive inquiry, they move far beyond story swapping to constructing new knowledge through solving problems of understanding. Progressive inquiry (Hakkarainen et al., 2004) includes the following:

- *Creating context:* Through explicitly creating a context, the issues being investigated are connected with deep principles of the knowledge domain in question and anchored in authentic, practical, and complex problems of the external world, or issues about which the participants generally care.
- *Engaging in question-driven inquiry:* An essential aspect of progressive inquiry is generating one's own problems and questions to guide the inquiry; without questions generated by the participants themselves, there cannot be a genuine process of inquiry. Questions that arise from one's own need to understand have a special value in the process of inquiry.
- *Generating working theories:* Constructing their own working theories helps inquirers to systematically use their background knowledge and become aware of their presuppositions. Progressive inquiry is aimed at the explication of these intuitive ideas.
- *Critical evaluation:* Critical evaluation underscores the need to assess the strengths and weaknesses of the tentative theories (explanations) produced so as to direct and regulate the evolution of inquiry. It is essential to focus on constructively evaluating the advancement of the inquiry process itself, rather than simply an end result.
- *Searching for new information:* Searching for and working with "research" is necessary for deepening one's understanding. New information can come from literature, consulting experts, or conducting one's own explorations. Explicit comparison of the intuitive working theories with the well-established ones makes the limitations of individual and collective knowledge apparent.
- *Engagement in deepening inquiry:* A critical condition for progress is that inquirers focus on improving their ideas by generating more specific questions and searching for new information. The dynamic nature of inquiry is supported by the fact that generating working theories and obtaining new research knowledge makes new guiding questions accessible.
- *Shared expertise:* The agent of knowledge creation is not an isolated individual but an individual embedded in a community, or even the community itself. All of the preceding aspects of inquiry can be shared with other inquirers. Inquiry can advance substantially through relying on socially distributed cognitive resources and collaborative efforts to enhance shared understanding.

Progressive inquiry in a learning networks framework has a context that is delimited by a needs-based learning focus, a recognized necessity of making the tacit explicit, and an understanding that new knowledge is constructed by considering teachers' personal beliefs and knowledge in relation to other sources of theory, research, and best practice. The last of the elements—shared expertise—hints at the collaborative power that is at the heart of learning networks. It is this intersection of collaboration and inquiry that defines true joint work of the sort that Little (1990) describes. As Schmoker (2004) explains, mere collegiality will not cut it. Discussion about curricular issues or popular goals can feel good but go nowhere. In our work (Earl & Katz, 2007), we have been able to differentiate collaborative inquiry—the substance of joint work—from the rest of collaboration. Collaborative inquiry centers on *learning* and includes things like the following:

- Monitoring and discussing activities or projects to learn from successful and from failed initiatives
- Engaging in systematic analysis of data
- Regularly drawing on research and/or outside expertise to improve practice
- Initiating intentional professional learning opportunities in relation to inquiry
- Regularly challenging one another's assumptions about teaching and learning
- Being receptive to feedback on teaching from school colleagues
- Talking openly with school colleagues about differing views, opinions, and values
- Dealing openly with professional conflicts that arise in the school

At the second literacy lead meeting, the teacher leaders were ready to develop a shared practical understanding of making inferences as a first step to their collaborative inquiry process.

Sheryl arrived at the next meeting of the literacy leads and was enthusiastically welcomed by three teachers who already knew her from the model lessons she had conducted in their schools. She knew a bit about the network from Mat when he contacted her to be sure she was attending the meeting. Sheryl had asked that he do a very brief introduction to the group and indicated that she preferred to act primarily as an observer for this first meeting.

Mat was the facilitator for this meeting and Rochelle was the secretary. Mat went around the table asking the literacy leads to share their discoveries about the strategies that the teachers in their schools were using to teach students to make inferences as a part of reading comprehension. As the teachers went around the room reporting their findings, Rochelle recorded the different strategies, including Think-Aloud, Directed Reading-Thinking, and Concept Mapping. There didn't seem to be any dominant approach and they were a bit surprised that many of the teachers said that they did not teach "making inferences" directly. They embedded it in their informal teaching as part of guided reading. Some even mused that making inferences was perhaps not a strategy in reading comprehension with which the teachers were really familiar.

Mat then invited the group to discuss the next steps, given that they didn't want a hit-and-miss process. They needed to have some kind of evidence that the strategies they selected were effective, and a planned approach to bringing their teachers on board as well.

> *As the group talked through the different strategies, it became evident that members even had a different understanding of the definition and role of making inferences in literacy learning. The more they discussed making inferences, the more confused they felt. Eventually, the frustration level of the literacy leads became palpable, and Mat suggested that they take a breather and remember that they did have access to expert support.*
>
> *Sheryl was quiet through the meeting and thought very intently about how the model lessons and debriefing conversations that she had conducted over the last two years had been very effective in targeting some of these questions, but that she had reached so few teachers. She knew that, for this group to be effective, the first thing members needed to do was to get on the same page and achieve a collective understanding of making inferences so they could start to recognize the strategies that best suited their schools' needs.*
>
> *When the literacy leads turned to her for help to guide their thinking, Sheryl suggested that the first step was to work collectively to develop a common understanding of how making inferences evolved in the curriculum from K–6. She suggested that they work together to learn more about making inferences and to come to a shared understanding, and maybe even a process that they all could use. Once a shared conceptual understanding was achieved, they could work on a process to connect the shared understanding to jointly and independently analyze student work.*
>
> *When the meeting was over, Mat confided to Rochelle that this was harder than he had expected. But he thought that the group was "up for it" and he personally would be happy to learn more about comprehension. He didn't feel much like an expert at the moment!*

COLLABORATIVE INQUIRY FOR TEACHER LEADERS

Collaborative inquiry is the mechanism for building the necessary practitioner capacity in relation to the learning focus. It provides an effective means for taking up the answer to the question, What is it that teachers need to learn in order to change classroom practice in a way that will respond to the student learning need? Put slightly differently, creating opportunities for focused collaborative inquiry is how the network meets its capacity-building obligations. It is the mechanism for practitioner learning, done collaboratively. Collaborative inquiry is a way of ensuring (or at least trying to ensure) that collaboration goes beyond casual story swapping and becomes true, intentional, joint work that results in new understandings that will move practice forward.

The network provides the structure for the requisite learning together to happen. Part of this involves determining "who" needs to be involved and "how." Real school improvement takes place one classroom at a time, but reaching all teachers matters. Remember, the network is a network of schools. Everyone in the school is in the network, although they are often represented by their colleagues. How can the network operate to create those job-embedded professional learning opportunities in relation to the focus? What do they look like? Who leads them? Formal leaders—the principals—are likely not the content leaders. They are the change-management leaders. They create the conditions for change and they manage the process of making it happen. They also distribute leadership, identifying those teacher leaders who are in a position to lead in the focus area because of their expertise, and then making the space for it to happen.

The network creates the structure and form for teacher leaders, identified as such because of their expertise in the defined focus area, to work and learn together and to engage their colleagues in their learning journey. They begin by understanding the student and the teacher learning demands in relation to the focus and becoming expert in the identified areas of focus. At the same time, they learn about the process for deepening professional knowledge and refining skills to work together with colleagues in their schools. So, what does collaborative inquiry for teacher leaders look like? There are several established methodologies that promote this kind of learning (e.g., action research, lesson study, and collaborative analysis of student work). When done in depth, all of these approaches can move teachers to an investigation of their own practices and consideration of other practices.

Over the next month, Sheryl guided and facilitated the curriculum activity with the teacher leaders to ensure that their collaboration would be in the form of joint work.

Once a week for four weeks, Sheryl gave the literacy leads a task they needed to complete together. They were asked to cull out making inferences from the curriculum standards; have structured discussions about their understanding of and experiences with making inferences; participate in debates about the content of articles on the components of reading comprehension; and finally, develop a map for their use in school. At the end of a month, the network of teacher leaders had developed a collective map of how making inferences evolved in the curriculum from K–6. Sheryl and the group of teacher leaders were impressed with the progress made in terms of their conceptual understanding of the focus and its place in literacy learning.

The next step for the group was to apply their conceptual understanding to analyze student work. Sheryl decided that this next step would require direct capacity building in the form of a training session with literacy leads. She asked each of the leads to bring a sample of student work that they could align to their collective map for the next session.

In Chapter 2 we talked about the complementary relationship between professional learning communities (PLCs) and NLCs. We suggested that NLCs are best thought of as networks of PLCs in schools. We also noted that many PLCs, while well-intentioned, are not focused enough to make an impact. In fact, they become activity traps, consuming a lot of energy and resource without any real outcome. One of the most powerful ways to ensure that any PLC stays focused—whether within or across schools—is by making sure that it is anchored by actual student work. The most focused PLC meetings we have experienced have been ones in which an actual piece of student work is on the table, with groups of teachers working together to consider it in relation to a particular learning demand. The process explicitly brings a curriculum expectation to the table (as specified by the network learning focus), considers the path of student learning in relation to the expectation, and examines the implications for teaching in relation to these dimensions. The student work samples that anchor the process are both learning cases and individual student improvement opportunities. They are learning cases in that the chosen examples are prototypes for learning about the expectation, the learning progression, and the high-leverage instructional strategies in relation to the focus. They also provide an individual student improvement opportunity insofar as the learning involved will (should) move each particular child under consideration forward in the focus area.

Having actual student work is at the center of the collaborative inquiry exercise. It creates the opportunity for evidence-driven, focused professional learning conversations. Elsewhere (Earl & Katz, 2006; Earl & Timperley, 2008) we have outlined the capacities involved in evidence-informed decision making and contrasted this mode of thought with the often quite well-established mental stance of "I know because I know!" We've already spoken a fair bit about using evidence to aim the work of school improvement. Collaborative analysis of actual student work—as an evidence-driven capacity-building opportunity—pushes the participants towards higher order forms of collaboration, the kind of joint work that challenges thinking and practice. Like Richard Elmore (2007), we have observed the sometimes disabling culture of "niceness" that permeates the fabric of all sorts of professional collaborations. Elmore describes the problem as follows:

> In the culture of American schools, there is a strong current of "niceness" that makes productive discussions of practice nearly impossible. People talk about their own practice and the practice of others in convoluted and obtuse ways, always accompanied by something superficially positive. Candor is essential. (p. 22)

Our research on learning networks (Earl & Katz, 2007) has identified the importance of moderate professional conflict as a key enabler of the kind of focused professional learning that changes thinking and practice, and that ultimately impacts on student achievement. As a practice, there are few more powerful catalysts of networked professional learning. It is important to understand that we're not talking about personal conflict, but rather the kind of professional conflict that places thinking and practice under scrutiny in a way that builds and refines understanding. Moderate professional conflict lies at the heart of collaborative inquiry, as tacit knowledge and understanding are made explicit through the kind of collaborative discourse that challenges thinking and practice. (Interestingly, the emergence of this kind of conflict is precisely when someone usually suggests taking a break in order to detach from an uncomfortable situation.) Learning networks work by creating opportunities for this kind of collaborative inquiry—the kind focused on actual student work that keeps the conversations centered on the substance that is the defined learning focus of the NLC. Candor is important. These conversations must transcend the superficially positive. At the same time, the "challenge" is about ideas and practices and must be separated from the person. It is essential to separate the person from the practice to transcend the pull towards the culture of niceness that inhibits real inquiry. Elmore (2007) shares his observations of the medical profession in which practitioners discuss problems of practice in relatively impersonal ways, as if their practices are detached from who they are. Educators, he argues, differ in that they tend to confuse the practice with the person, and this creates a problem. As he puts it:

> It is hard to change your practice when your practice is central to your personal identity. Every change becomes a challenge to who you are, in some basic sense. In general, professionals can't afford this confusion of the practice with the person because they live in a world in which practices are changing rapidly in response to new knowledge and new problems. (p. 23)

Elmore (2007) suggests the utility of protocols in encouraging the separation of person from practice. Protocols keep the focus of the conversation on the practice. We have come across a variety of different protocols to guide the collaborative analysis of student work.

The CASL Process

Background: A teacher brings forward a student work sample in the area of the student learning focus for the network. She provides relevant background information about the student and describes the desired learning outcomes for the piece of work. She also describes the instruction, experiences, and activities (teaching and logistics) that preceded the work product that is the sample, as well as the accompanying rationale. The teacher explains why she chose this particular work sample in relation to the focus.

Observation: Members of the group examine the work sample on their own and then share their observations. The observation stage is descriptive. It is designed to generate a body of evidence for the analysis. The temptation to be evaluative or diagnostic is typically high, but it is important to develop a descriptive voice prior to making any judgments.

Analysis: In the analysis stage, the participants investigate both learning and teaching patterns. First, the group makes determinations about what the student understands and can do, as well as about gaps or misconceptions that are apparent. On the pedagogical side, the

(Continued)

(Continued)

analysis generates learning conversations about the effectiveness of particular instructional strategies, and focuses on the usefulness of the assignment that gave rise to the work sample as a vehicle for making student thinking and understanding explicit.

Planning next steps: The group discusses what both the student and the teacher need to do next by planning a short-term student learning goal, including a rationale for why this is the sensible direction, as well as the kind of detail and specificity that says if I do x, my student is likely to get better at y because . . . Finally, they decide when this student's work sample will be brought back and the inquiry is explicitly broadened to consider the implications of the learning from the CASL session (about the focus) for other students.

One that we've found to be useful is an adaptation of Langer, Colton, and Goff's (2003) Collaborative Analysis of Student Learning (CASL) model. The CASL protocol involves systematically working through a set of questions as a group, with the presenting teacher taking the lead. In this way, the learning opportunity extends to include both the content related to the focus and the process for supporting collaborative inquiry. If collaborative inquiry is the engine that drives professional learning in networks, then actual evidence is the fuel for the machine.

At the next meeting, Sheryl wanted to guide the group from collaborating to collaborative inquiry using student work as the point of practical interest. Sheryl also believed that a spotlight on student work would facilitate the group's work in achieving the learning expectations outlined with its role for the network.

Sheryl decided to model a Collaborative Analysis of Student Learning (CASL) session for the leads so that they could learn about the approach and inquiry methodology within the context of what it means to teach and learn skills in making inferences in schools. This would be a practical way to work through the leads' differences in applied understanding of making inferences.

Raymond and Mat offered to bring in two samples of student work that would illustrate two different levels of knowledge and skills in making inferences, as made evident by their group-developed K–6 Inference in the Curriculum guide. Sheryl explained the CASL process to the group and identified herself as the facilitator of the session and Raymond as the first teacher requesting CASL support. She explained that, in the future, the literacy leads would be in her role (as facilitator) in their schools as they led their teachers through this same process.

Sheryl: Raymond, you have a piece of student work. Can you tell us about the background to the sample?

Raymond: Well, I am working with Grade 4 students and I have two student samples from an activity that I tried with my class in an attempt to help them make inferences. I selected the work based on what I thought I knew about my students' current skills and how I could get them to really practice their skills. I was a little stumped by these two students. They are both enthusiastic, but they are not very good at making inferences independently. So I decided to develop some questions with multiple answers for the kids to consider. Kind of drawing on multiple choice and then asking them to tell me why they chose their answer and if there was something else that they could say about the statement.

This first example is Freeda's answer to one of the questions. You can see that she simply does not infer well and then she jumps to predictions. We have gone over and over this a lot in class using many examples. But she just does not get it.

Sheryl: Okay—so is there some background about Freeda that would help us better understand her work?

Raymond: She is just an average student. She usually does okay on her work and achieves the expectations. She usually does not have a problem with the work and she does understand the text without too many problems. She has a great imagination and creates stories—she predicts well too because she does see different possibilities. But making an inference is just a challenge for her.

Mat: Well, I like the idea of using the multiple choices to support their learning. I think that it is a neat approach. But Freeda is not really getting it.

Raymond: No, she is not.

Sheryl: Let's stick to the protocol. After background, we need to go through observations, analysis, and then next steps. So for now, we should focus on collecting our observations. Right now, each of you should read through the student work sample and write out your observations. Then we will talk about them.

The group wrote out their observations as they read through the student work sample Raymond had given each of them. When they were done, Sheryl invited each group member to contribute their observations. Many of the observations focused on Freeda's answers. The group noticed how she always drew a conclusion and made a prediction about the next piece of the story. The prediction was always about making the situation better for the main character.

After the group members were done sharing their observations, Sheryl invited the group to focus on the learning and teaching patterns that they had noticed.

Rochelle: Well, I don't know that all of the questions are really at a Grade 4 level. For example, when I look at question 5, I would categorize this as a Grade 3 question.

Mat: Is that important? Either way, Freeda did not get the right answer.

Rochelle: I do think that it is important because not only is she not really able to identify which part of her thinking is making an inference, but she is not able to do the Grade 3 level work in making inferences. And most questions are harder than this one.

Raymond:	Maybe that is one question that was easier, but not all of them are.
Mat:	Hang on, I think that what Rochelle said about Freeda not identifying which part of her thinking is inference is important.
Raymond:	What do you mean?
Mat:	I am not sure. Rochelle, what did you mean by it?
Rochelle:	Well, I think that the multiple choice is confusing the student and not helping her. If you look at her written responses—especially the predictions—then you can see that she is making inferences.
Raymond:	But that is my point. I can see that. That is why I broke it down for her into bite-size pieces of inferences with the multiple choice. She is making inferences because her predictions make sense. But she can't tell me what they are—she just jumps.
Rochelle:	But you never ask her to do that here. You give her a bunch of choices and ask her to choose. She is choosing based on what she knows and imagines. This is a problem with the strategy, not with the student.
Mat:	What do you suggest?
Rochelle:	A think-aloud where you record her answers in a formatted worksheet that identifies her responses as inference, conclusion, and predictions. You can guide her through it. I have been pushing this strategy in my school and one teacher is trying it. I have been present for three of the sessions, and it is really working. By the end, the kids are identifying their thinking in their own words.

The team continued to move from analysis to next steps. It repeated the process with Mat and then debriefed the process and its potential use in members' schools.

Sheryl stressed the importance of respecting the protocol. She discussed the importance of keeping the conversation professional and evidence informed through sticking to the parameters of the guidelines. When she was convinced the literacy leads appreciated the importance of this characteristic of the CASL process, she had the literacy leads start to plan and schedule their CASL school-implementation strategy.

WITHIN-SCHOOL FOCUSED PROFESSIONAL LEARNING: COLLABORATIVE INQUIRY FOR TEACHERS

The image of what it means to build capacity in focused collaborative inquiry through the network CASL sessions gives an image of what needs to be built and supported in schools. The goal in schools is structured opportunities for individual teachers to deepen their professional learning through collaborative examinations of their practices and of their own students' work in the focus area. We recently completed a development and research project designed to learn about what it takes to build teacher capacity in evidence-informed decision making and, by extension, what it takes to facilitate the development of this competence. A key finding was that teachers really need to see their *own* students in the data (Katz, Earl, & Dack, 2008). Structured CASL sessions at the school level provided the venue for the kind of focused collaborative inquiry that appropriates the work of the network at the school level with inherent teacher ownership of the learning and improvement agenda. The idea behind this approach is that each teacher selects a focus student as a professional learning anchor case, as in the network CASL session. Because of the capacity building work that has unfolded in the network, the literacy leads are well positioned to lead the learning. As with the network CASL sessions, the benefits of the process are twofold. First, there is the obvious opportunity to move a particular student forward. Second, the student provides the job-embedded venue for professional learning in relation to the focus that can be taken back to the classroom and extrapolated to support the learning of all students.

All the literacy leads were now running CASL sessions in their schools. They downloaded the strategy from the network to their schools in order to build capacity with the teachers in their schools using relevant local data—real student work.

Mat and Raymond are two literacy leads in different schools in the network. Mat invited Raymond to join him for the first CASL session that he was facilitating in his school. He was working with a group of Grade 3 and 4 teachers, and he wanted to receive immediate feedback on his process from someone with experience. That week, Sheryl was already busy supporting Nancy and Reza, two other literacy leads in the network, and Mat did not want to postpone his first CASL session. He asked his principal to arrange with Joan (Raymond's principal) so that Raymond would be able to join their session.

Reena volunteered to be the first teacher to have a CASL session when Mat introduced the concept in the all-staff meeting. She had been struggling with a male student in her Grade 4 class who had arrived with very low inference skills. Last year, Christian achieved a Level 3 on the provincial assessment—he met provincial standards. However, a closer look at his results indicated that he was at a Level 1 on the section of reading comprehension for making inferences. Reena had been working with the whole class on

Name: Christian

When I read

Name of book: Only a Cow

These words from the text: "Well we could do something different for a change. Something exciting."

"Lucille, we're only cows. Cows aren't exciting," said Bertha.

make me think that: The cows are bored. They wants to do more stuff. They want to play and not eat all the time.

because: The cows are talking about just eating. My mom makes me stop playing to eat.

reading comprehension and had recently focused her attention on skills for making inferences. Christian was still having some difficulties with anything that was not linear and explicit in the text.

Raymond, Mat, Reena, Sana, and Sophie were present at the CASL session. Sana and Sophie taught Grade 3 and 4 at the same school. Reena introduced Christian's background and explained that she was working with him using a scaffolding tool that most of her other students were no longer using. It was a guide to help Christian pull out sentences from the stories he was reading and relate the text to something in his own life. The template was simple, and Christian was using it. Reena explained that her objective was to get Christian to think about the text in terms of his own experiences and then ask questions about the storyline.

The group of teachers read through the unit and examined three of Christian's "When I read" products. They reported their observations to Reena. Mat had to intervene only once to redirect the discussion to focus on observation when Sana offered a suggestion for improving the practice. Mat explained that Next Steps was the last step in the CASL protocol. The group continued with their analysis after they completed their observations.

Sana: Well, it seems that Christian is able to relate to the story.

Sophie: I agree. You can see with the Cow example that he is able to make a link with being bored and eating.

Sana: Yes, but he is not quite there yet because he is thinking in terms of being bored rather than being boring.

Mat: Hmm. The objective is for Christian to relate to the story and then start to question the direction of the story. So, for him, being bored might be the equivalent of not playing. That is how it is in his boy world. Eating is boring—he is boring when he is bored.

Sana: So, he is expressing it in his reality.

Mat: Yes.

Sophie: But what he is not doing is developing questions that ask about the direction of the story.

Mat: No, it does not seem that he is doing that.

Reena: Most of the students are now at that stage of learning where they are predicting. Christian does not really make contributions in those discussions.

Sana: And you said that you already conducted a think-aloud with him where you modeled the questioning?

Reena: Yes.

Mat: You did this only once, right?

Reena: Yes, but I have other students and that was all the time I could offer him.

Sophie: When I look at your scaffolding document, I notice that you ask Christian to relate the text to his own experiences. But you really don't ask him about the next piece of the story.

Reena: We did that in class—that is what the think-aloud showed. He is supposed to take the text, and tell me what it makes him think of and why. They are supposed to include the next part of the story in that response too!

Mat: But Christian is not getting that part.

Reena: No. And I really don't see why because we have gone over it with different methods in the classroom. Most of the kids get it. They are curious about the story—Christian is not. He waits for the story to come to him and does not wonder about what is going to happen next.

Sophie: Then maybe he needs more scaffolding in the tool.

Sana: Maybe all it will take is another question on the tool. So that you add the question about the next part of the story at the end.

Sophie: You mean something like, "What do you think will happen next in the story?"

Sana: Well, that is a prediction question. I think that the objective is to get Christian to ask questions about the story, right?

Reena: Yes.

Mat: So what about something like, "What question about the story does this make you think of?"

Reena: I can do that. I don't have a problem with it, but when does Christian get weaned off of this scaffolding tool? The other students are already not using it and I am about to expand this one for him.

Mat: Well, if he needs it, he needs it.

Sana: But maybe he does not need it all anymore. It seems like he can relate the text to his own experiences. The last two pieces from him show that he gets it.

Reena: In class, he articulates links. They are sometimes weak—but they are there in his own language.

Mat: Sana, where are you going with this?

Sana: Should you try to modify the tool so that it no longer scaffolds the relating objective and focuses on your actual objective: to ask questions about the story?

Mat: Huh. Yes, that seems like a reasonable step forward. But maybe Christian needs to develop his own story to become curious about what happens next. Maybe he does not know that there can be a lot of different ways a story can develop.

The conversation continued as the group discussed the different ways in which Christian's understanding of inference could be supported. At the end of the meeting, Reena agreed to modify the scaffolding tool, model it for all the students, and post it on the wall so that the students knew what to ask themselves when they were reading. For Christian and other students finding it challenging, she would offer them an individual copy to complete. They agreed that, in a month, Reena would meet with the group again with Christian's work. She also agreed to work with Mat on developing a lesson on how to create a different ending to a story that could be linked with the questioning tool.

The session ended with a group discussion on the process and the teachers left for their classes. Raymond and Mat remained in the class to debrief the CASL process and how it related to Mat's literacy leadership in the school. They talked through the observations that Raymond had made and the feedback that would be useful for their network group.

Time for Reflection

Describe an occasion where student learning needs prompted you to engage in new learning yourself. How did you come to realize that you needed to learn something new? What evidence did you have of student learning needs? How did your learning unfold?

How would you find out about the tacit knowledge of people in your group ("what we know")? What sources would you go to determine what is already known in an area of interest ("what is known")?

Have you ever participated in collaborative inquiry? What were you investigating? Who was involved? What role did you play? How was the outcome different from your original position?

7

Using the Network to Support Professional Learning for Leaders

In the last chapter, we unpacked what it means for student learning to signal teacher learning. We also looked at what learning for teachers actually entails if it is to move beyond the ineffective one-shot workshop model (Darling-Hammond & Richardson, 2009) and become truly "job-embedded." Teacher practice influences student learning and achievement, but practice does not really change unless the *understanding* that is the foundation on which the practice is built changes as well. That said, professional learning doesn't only mean teacher learning. It also means leader learning. Leadership practices enable the necessary teacher learning. Or, to turn it around slightly, teacher learning needs suggest leader learning needs. The question at the heart of this chapter is, What does it mean for leaders to learn so that they can practice in ways that support the necessary job-embedded teacher learning?

COLLABORATIVE INQUIRY AND FOCUSED LEARNING FOR LEADERS

Identifying student learning needs will not mean much if teachers can't answer the "so what" question: What will help this student learn? What is it that teachers need to learn to change their practice in ways that will respond to student learning needs? School administrators, as formal leaders, are challenged to create the conditions by which their schools can become the kind of learning communities that support focused professional learning for teachers that will change classroom practice. This challenge defines leader learning. It matters because learning for leaders enables learning for teachers that, in turn, enables learning for students.

The network provides the space to merge the learning of the lead teachers and the administrators with a particular purpose in mind—to advance the capacity-building agenda in both the process and content areas back at the school. In the early stages, once the focus is established, the network-level work for the administrators and the lead teachers unfolds in separate structures as each group pursues a learning agenda (and format) that relates to a different dimension of the focus. Administrators typically begin with the process learning related to creating the conditions for establishing learning-driven schools, while lead teachers begin with the learning demands that are given by the content of the focus. This learning priority differentiation is sensible in that between-group expertise is distributed. Administrators are expected to be the change-management experts; lead teachers are expected to be the content experts. That said, neither can improve schools without the other. Administrators are not expected to be the content experts, but they do need to know enough about the content to understand the necessary professional learning demands for teachers (and students) and to be able to identify and leverage the content expertise of the informal leaders. Content experts do not have the formal responsibility for moving the whole-school agenda forward, but they need to know enough about cultivating the conditions for change to situate the content learning. When it comes to actually moving schools forward, the interdependence of both learning priority areas becomes clear. Focused collaborative inquiry and focused instructional leadership, as the key enablers of professional knowledge creation and sharing, merge both content and process.

The networks with which we work use a variety of structures and strategies for bringing the administrator and lead teacher components of the network together. In some networked learning communities (NLCs), the principals join the lead teacher learning sessions once they are up and running. In other networks, select lead teachers attend the administrator sessions and act as boundary spanners across the groups. In still others, the principals and lead teachers arrange their network meetings so that they are at the same time and in the same place so that they can begin separately and then join together in the last hour for concrete next-step planning back at the schools. And, in the case of some very mature networks, the network meetings are planned and blended together, and then separated as needed based on the agenda.

In Selkirk, Joan (principal) and Raymond (literacy lead) used their professional learning community (PLC) to practically merge the learning in each network group. They wanted to make sure that their local processes were fostering professional knowledge creation and sharing.

Joan was aware of the work and progress of the literacy leads. She had modified the PLC meetings at her school so that they adopted the network learning focus. Every second week, the PLC discussion was about developing practical strategies to link the work being done at the network level to the work being done in the school. The meetings were becoming more popular with the staff, and the two Grade 3 teachers had become regular participants in the lunch PLC.

Over time, the exchange of information and discussions about connecting the work of the network to the schools became a key process in bringing in new ideas. Joan and Raymond acted as key boundary spanners in the network because they not only carried over information from the network to the schools, but also stayed in close contact with one another to be sure that the messages from the principal and the literacy network groups were consistent for their teachers.

In one PLC discussion, Raymond explained that the literacy leads were developing a common observation tool to help them identify the teaching practices that appeared to be significant in improving making inferences. He described the way that he used it for his own learning and said the literacy leads were planning to use it with the teachers in the schools. In their own school, Riz and Rewall were just about to try their first joint conversation over student work.

Joan: I really like the idea of a common tool and I am wondering whether it can be helpful for alignment across the network.

Raymond: We started to talk about that at the last literacy leads meeting and we were a little stumped by how to proceed with the tool on a larger scale. So we dropped it for now.

Joan: Perhaps the principal group can take a look at it as a potential tool to help us monitor change across the schools.

Raymond: I'm not sure we're ready for that yet.

Riz: I don't think that you can use the observation tool to help teachers improve their teaching and evaluate them at the same time. It simply does not work.

Joan: I did not mean for it to be an evaluation. I meant it to be a means to collect some data about what we are doing so that we can look it over and maybe do some checks on our improvement program.

The conversation continued as the PLC group talked about ways to make teachers feel safe while monitoring their practices by keeping everything attached to the focus and moving away from evaluative methods. They were in the middle of an intense dialogue about improvement and collecting data when lunchtime finished. They all agreed to think more about it and come back to the conversation at the next PLC meeting with more insights.

The network administrators and teacher leaders are charged with the task of learning how schools can appropriate or download the learning of the network. As you might imagine, there are myriad possible ways for this to unfold. One network with which we work asks teacher leaders and administrators to independently articulate what each needs from the other in order to practice instructional leadership effectively. They recognize that the work of focused improvement involves an interdependence of roles whereby content expertise (teacher leaders) and process expertise (administrators) are codependent. The teacher leaders have the capacity to lead the required professional learning back at the school (having built an understanding of the content-based learning demands through the work of the network), but the administrators have to lead (and sanction) the development and embedding of the necessary structures that will support true job-embedded professional learning.

Regardless of the specifics of any particular networked-learning meeting, it is important not to lose sight of the fact that the reason for NLCs is to move forward in two places and on two dimensions. The two places are (1) the network, and (2) the school. The two dimensions are (1) in relation to the focus, and (2) in relation to the "enabling" processes and practices of focused professional learning. Each of the dimensions needs to be embedded in each of the places. Structured protocols can serve as useful scaffolds for keeping the NLC on this course.

The principal group decided to systematize a school–network monitoring mechanism in its meetings. The principals wanted to engage in a consistent practice that helped them reflect on their efforts and progress.

Joan was excited about the work being done in her school to connect the work of the literacy leads and the principals in the network. So when the principals' group agreed that all its meetings would begin with each principal completing a reflective diary as part of the network protocol, she was confident that her school efforts would show she was creating good conditions in her school to move the focus forward.

Given the success of protocols to date, the principal group naturally developed a reflective diary template to make sure that they were meeting their objectives with the reflective diaries. They wanted to have a template that made them check whether they were (1) working at both the school and network levels, and (2) consciously focusing and balancing their efforts appropriately. The goal was to make sure that they had the data so that they could analyze it and redirect their action to make sure that no cell was being ignored.

Questions	*In your school*	*In your network*
1. What have you done in relation to the *focus*?		
2. What have you done in terms of creating the *conditions* for focused *professional learning*?		
3. What have you done in terms of *monitoring* and *assessing* progress?		

Over time, the principals collected their completed protocols. The collection of these documents provided the raw material to discuss their priorities and orient inquiry at both the school and network levels. After two months of using the diary approach to start meetings, Carl asked the group to review its progress using the collection of completed diaries. The principals dedicated a meeting to reviewing the documents and finding patterns in their work.

Each principal was responsible for reviewing the collection of completed diaries of a partner. The principal would read through all of the text in one cell (e.g., What have you done in relation to the focus "In your school"?) and then write a statement about the pattern they noticed over time. They created summary statements for all six cells. When the summarizing was completed, the partnered principals discussed and compared their notes, trying to find patterns of progress and issues. Finally, the principals shared their findings in a whole-group discussion.

During the discussion of their progress, everyone was impressed by the amount of work that was accomplished in some of the schools, and less impressed by what was achieved in others.

Carl: I think that we could work on our coherence. Some of you have jumped into the work but others are stalled. I think we need a strategy for moving forward together. I like the philosophy that our literacy leads have adopted. They don't consider themselves successful unless all of the schools show improvement. That is the philosophy we need to adopt.

Elsie: I agree. I'll speak as one of the "stalled" group. I am just having trouble getting things moving. And, even though my teachers seem to be in favor of our focus, they don't seem to see the focus as a reason to change something in their classroom practice. I'm not even sure my literacy lead is convinced that anything needs to change.

Joan: Then maybe you need a direct approach to how you are monitoring the progress?

Elsie: Why would I monitor progress when I know that there won't be any?! I am trying to create the conditions for focused professional learning, but the teachers are not biting.

Joan:	I noticed that in reading your summary. But maybe your teachers need a more forceful approach so that they will bite. Monitoring can serve that purpose.
Charles:	I know that it can serve that purpose, but is that how we want to approach our professional teachers? If we force their hand, then aren't we doing the focus a disservice?
Joan:	What do you mean?
Charles:	Well, it seems to me that monitoring and evaluation are really regarded as punitive measures. They are the pressure mechanisms that have negative impact.
Rita:	Whoa! I know that is true in some cases, but we have never once talked about evaluation of our teachers. We have always talked about monitoring so that we can have some data for working in our cycle of inquiry.
Charles:	I agree. But just because that is how *we* are working with it, and that is a sincere approach on our side, it does not mean that the teachers will ever see it that way.
Joan:	But if we don't show them something different, then how will they know that there is a different way of working with results that can be helpful for their work?

The conversation continued as the group members realized they had stumbled into an issue that was potentially causing friction on the ground. The group did not end the conversation in agreement on the approach or in their beliefs about monitoring, pressure, and encouraging teachers. But they did come to three agreements.

First, the principals needed to bring in expertise to help them better understand how monitoring, motivation, and change functioned in their schools so they could capitalize on the research that had already been done in educational reform. Second, the principals needed to take their own summaries back to their schools and use them to discuss direction and strategies with their own leadership teams. Finally, the principal and literacy lead groups needed to engage in a joint, structured discussion about the results of the reflective diary summaries and next steps.

USING CRITICAL FRIENDS TO PROMOTE INQUIRY AND FOCUS EFFORTS

The network provides the learning context within which school leaders can engage in the kind of collaborative inquiry that yields useful professional learning. The "critical friend" concept plays an important role here. Although it sounds like an oxymoron, the idea of critical friends is an important and powerful one. Friends bring a high degree of positive regard, are forgiving, and are tolerant of shortcomings. Critics are challenging, often conditional, and intolerant of failure. Critical friends offer both support and critique in an open, honest appraisal (MacBeath, 1998). They can observe what may not be apparent to insiders, facilitate reflection on issues, ask questions, probe for justification and evidence to support perceptions, and help reformulate interpretations. They are not afraid to challenge assumptions, beliefs, or simplistic interpretations, and they do so in a nonjudgmental and helpful way. Critical friends can remind participants of what they have accomplished and facilitate their movement toward the next steps (Earl & Katz, 2006).

There are myriad possibilities when it comes to potential critical friends because critical friendship is about function, not formal position. Critical friends can be external or internal to the system. Key district personnel can think about their relationships with schools in this way, though this kind of role definition is not without challenge. We say this because, in the context of existing formal relationships between actors within a school system, critical friendship is not so much a role definition as it is a role *re*definition. For one thing, power differentials attached to formal roles and responsibilities between, say, superintendents and principals, or principals and teachers, make true critical friendship in these relationships a challenge to achieve. Opening up your practices to scrutiny, working to explicitly know what you don't know, taking risks in the service of innovation, and so on are not typically the kinds of things you look to do in the context of any kind of superior/subordinate relationship. Such power dichotomies are often situated within an atmosphere of judgment and surveillance. When you attempt to redefine these interrelations in ways that are consistent with the spirit of critical friendships, it is not uncommon to face the kind of fear expressed in questions like, "How can we keep this from being used against us in some way?" or "Why would we give them the hatchet that they'll use to give us the ax?" (Holcomb, 1999, p. 23).

These responses are real and they are powerful. We can't ignore them. They need to be taken up, engaged with, and worked through. Our work suggests that the root of these responses is a psychological condition that we might term the *imposter syndrome.* Essentially, the imposter syndrome is that little inner voice that we all carry around that whispers something like, "I have no idea how it is that I came to be doing what I'm doing but hopefully nobody will find me out!" Explicit acknowledgment of the existence and the pervasiveness of the imposter syndrome is one of the important keys to disabling its detrimental effects. The other is an overt recognition that while ignorance might be bliss, it's not particularly helpful in the service of new learning. Indeed, real new learning has as its prerequisite a conscious acknowledgment of what one doesn't know. It's Plato's paradox all over again. You have to know that you don't know in order to know, so to speak. In the same way that good classroom assessment asks children to make what they don't know explicit so that we can best tailor and target our instructional support, we also need to cultivate this kind of awareness with each other as adult learners. Critical friendship, at its heart, is designed to do just this.

At the next meeting, the principals recognized that they were too close to the work in their schools. They wanted a trusted person to help them gain perspective and understanding about their school's efforts and progress in meeting the expectations of their focus. They needed a critical friend.

When they met again, the principals were more aware of what was going on in each of their schools, but they were also more uncertain about how deep the focus was really going in classrooms. They expressed a desire to know the extent of progress their schools had made on the key features of building a network. They already knew that there were changes in practice in the teaching of strategies targeting making inferences from their literacy leads. But they wanted a critical eye that would help them target modifications and improvements in their local approaches.

Joan: I would like someone to come to my school and ask questions and reflect with my team on site to help us find our areas of improvement with respect to developing our part of the network.

Rita: I would like that too, but I want someone that is already familiar with the group and the work that we have done and the efforts we have made.

Rikard: Agreed. And I know that Carl is the critical friend for this group, but I don't want an evaluation of my efforts.

Joan: That is funny considering our talk about monitoring and evaluation! I guess we don't really like it either—there is just a lot of history tied to using results for oversight instead of improvement!

Rikard: Indeed!

Charles: Are you suggesting we all go to each other's schools? That is a lot of visits. I can't commit to that many.

Rikard: That is true—it would be too much.

Carl: I think that it would be too much for any one person to visit all schools and I agree with Rikard that it shouldn't be me. Input from each other would be valuable. What if we developed a schedule where each of you visits one school? This would mean that each of you would be a critical friend once and receive a critical friend to your school once.

Rita: I think that is very reasonable. I can certainly be in charge of one visit.

Rikard: Agreed. But when we come to the school, do we visit classes and talk to the literacy lead and some other teachers?

Joan: I think that could be a good idea. But do we want just an open visit like that? I am not sure that is going to get us the targeted feedback that we are looking for.

Charles: So, what is it that the visits are about?

Elsie: They are about seeing how a school is doing at being part of the network.

Rikard: I think that it is more about how the school is using the network ideas to advance the focus. So how are the teachers and leadership in the school working together?

	This is about how the teacher learning is being supported and monitored rather than a focus on the student learning.
Rita:	Kind of like a targeted look at the process in the school.
Charles:	Yes, I think that is it.
Joan:	Then we should have a common way of doing these visits.
Elsie:	And maybe have a common way of preparing for the visits too. I mean, my leadership team is so busy working on the focus that it is not stopping to reflect on the way we are working all the time.
Rita:	I think we are all in the same boat on that one. That is what these visits are intended to promote.
Carl:	So, then, what does it look like?
Joan:	Well, the best thing to do is to go back to the basics that we are working from— the key enablers of real new learning. Should we start with those?
Elsie:	We could. But I think that we need more than just going through the enablers. We need a template that guides us through some critical questions that we ask of ourselves and that the critical friend asks of us. That way the school is prepared, and the critical friend knows what to look for.
Rikard:	That is a good idea. This way, if there are areas that the school wants the critical friend to look more into, then we can focus attention at the school level.
Joan:	In that case, we should develop a template that the school can use to prepare, and then that is what they go through with the critical friend during the visit.
Rita:	Sounds good. In that case, just frame the template in terms of questions that are directly related to each of those key enablers.
Charles:	Okay—who is going to develop this thing?
Joan:	I have something in mind. I will take a crack at it if I can get two more sets of eyes to work with me.
Carl:	I have done countless school visits and supported school leadership teams— maybe this is where my expertise can best be used. I can review the template and help focus the questions.
Rita:	Yes, I think that it is better for you to help with the template than to do site visits. And this way we can get a chance to see one another's schools and meet the leadership teams and other literacy leads.
Elsie:	If you'd like, I can take a look with you and help develop part of it.

The group decided that Joan, Elsie, and Carl would work together over the next week to develop a plan that would include a template for the critical friend network visits and a tentative schedule of visits. They would circulate the documents and, with the whole group's feedback, a final plan would be in place.

Collaborative inquiry makes a difference because it is a methodology that makes beliefs and practices explicit, and subsequently open to challenge. In that process, critical friends play a key role. People do not wake up each morning and go out into the world with the purpose of finding ways to be "uncomfortable" through challenge. In fact, it's usually the opposite; they are more likely to preserve and conserve the status quo. But dissonance and disequilibrium are critical prerequisites to real new learning. It is hard to get there alone. People need help. They need trusted others to help push them outside their comfort zones, but within safe environments. Administrators in learning networks are well positioned to play this critical friend role for one another. Scaffolding this important relationship in NLCs requires concerted effort.

Each school engaged in the critical friend site visit and interview to gain insight into their process and progress. This level of collaborative inquiry created a space for professional knowledge creation within the schools.

The critical friend school-to-school interview process consists of two parts: a getting-ready portion and the actual interview. Elsie and Carl organized the principals into critical friend pairs in a cascading arrangements so that Joan would visit Elsie, Elsie would visit Charles, Charles would visit Rita, Rita would visit Rikard, and Rikard would visit Joan. Each principal being "interviewed" was to meet first with key school staff to "get ready" for the critical friend school visit/interview. At the "get ready" meeting, the interviewee principal was responsible for leading a structured discussion on (1) the network learning focus in the school; (2) leadership in the school (formal, distributed, instructional); (3) relationships among school staff with respect to the network focus; (4) collaborative activities of staff in relation to the focus; (5) the use of research and evidence in making decisions (inquiry); and (6) professional learning opportunities as part of the network. Encouraging these kinds of focused in-school conversations would be the first benefit of the critical friend school-to-school interviews.

Elsie had volunteered to be the first to receive a critical friend. She used the document that she had developed with Carl to ensure that she was ready to go through the structured conversation with Joan. Joan arrived at Elsie's school and started her critical friend visit with a meeting that included Elsie the principal, Sophie the vice principal, and Rochelle the literacy lead for West Chelsy Elementary. Elsie had given a copy of the completed document to Joan three days before the visit. Everyone around the table had previously agreed that working through the document would be the best way to ensure they addressed all the important key features of effective learning communities.

The following are two excerpts of the group discussion that took place around the site visit preparation document. The first excerpt is from the part of the discussion where the group talked through Purpose and Focus; the second is when the group talked through Collaboration.

To what extent is our focus fostering new thinking and changes in practices in the school?

The focus has really taken hold in the school. The teachers are working together to improve how kids infer text. The literacy lead has conducted workshops and the teachers are really thinking about how to implement the new techniques in their daily practice.

Example

I was walking to my car at the end of the day and I overheard two of my teachers in a conversation with the literacy lead in the parking lot. One of the teachers was talking about how she was really anxious about making a "think-aloud" work in her class with three of her Grade 4 students who were struggling with asking questions about the story, given their prior knowledge.

What else do we need to know to understand this focus better?

We need to know how to use the strategies effectively in a classroom where there is such a range of skills among the twenty students.

How can we tell which teachers really understand the focus and which ones are superficially using the new terminology?

Are we still respecting the focus when we support kids who are still struggling with explicit comprehension skills like being able to retell the story?

Example

Teachers are struggling with the focus on inference because some of them would like to spend time on finding the meaning in the text and recreating the story. We need to better understand how the focus relates to all dimensions of literacy and the teachers need to appreciate the relationship between inference and student achievement and progress.

Elsie:	Well, as you can see, the focus seems to have really taken hold. I think that the teachers really get it and that they are committed to it. You might even say that the challenge that we are facing is that the teachers feel they have to really privilege inference at the expense of the rest of the elements of literacy.
Joan:	From what is written here, it seems that the teachers feel the students are not all ready for the push on inference. Is that a fair way of putting it?
Elsie:	Yes, I think so. So I think that we need to explore the role of inference in literacy so the teachers can really understand how to privilege it without sacrificing the rest of the parts.
Joan:	Are they sacrificing the rest of the parts?
Elsie:	What do you mean?
Joan:	Well, I don't know. When you looked at the literacy results, inference was not done well. That is why it became our focus. So it makes sense if the teachers are now spending more time on it because that is the weakness. I think what I am trying to say is that teachers might be uncomfortable with the shift in emphasis because it is something that they simply have not been emphasizing in their classes before. So they might not be able to see the gaps in inference as quickly as they can see them in decoding and . . . well, they have less experience with them too.

Elsie: That is a good point. And that could be true, but I don't know.

Rochelle: I think it is true. But they are getting a lot of training. The teachers are not resistant to the new ideas. They are simply trying to make them fit in with their current practices. Of course, this means a struggle with trying to find the time for it.

Sophie: I would agree with Rochelle in saying that there is goodwill amongst the teachers. But I don't know that it is a question of not enough time. I think maybe the teachers are worried that if they emphasize inference, the kids will score lower on the other elements of literacy that we have done well on in the past.

Elsie: So maybe it is a question of needing to see success.

Rochelle: I think it is a question of teachers really thinking that we are taking inference as a separate piece and they are losing sight of the fact that this tree is part of a forest.

Joan: If that is the case, then how do you make sure that the teachers recognize the important place of inference in literacy?

Sophie: Maybe we need a map

Rochelle: What do you mean?

Sophie: Well, it might help to have a visual where we put up all the components of literacy from the literacy test and curriculum and then have the teachers draw the relationships. We can post the concept map in the staffroom and refer to it when we engage in conversation about literacy.

Rochelle: Hmmm. That could work. We could build on the K−6 Making Inferences in the curriculum map we already have from the literacy lead group.

Joan: Why in the staffroom?

Sophie: So that the teachers are always seeing it and it is sinking in.

Joan: One of the things I'm noticing about the conversation on focus is that it is all about teachers. But there are other people in the school. There are students, parents, librarians, cleaning staff, administrative staff, etc. The school focus needs to be something that is understood by the whole school.

The conversation continued as the school group members talked through their impression that the whole school did indeed know and respect the focus. They were committed to sharing the focus widely, and even had a parents' night to explain it. Joan continuously asked what kind of evidence the group had for its beliefs.

They continued through the document, discussing how to respond to the questions with Joan and what kind of evidence counted as good evidence, then moving through to the Collaboration section.

To what extent does the notion of "our kids" exist in the school and network, as opposed to "my kids"?

The notion of "our kids" is not really taking hold in the school. There is still a sense of *my* kids and *my* class and what *I* do. There is little talk about what *we* do. Again, the exceptions are in Grades 2 and 4—but that is grade specific.

Example

When the teachers are talking in the workshops, they are talking about their kids and their work. The language that they use in the staffroom is "my kids" language. There is no sense of a single community of kids.

How does collaboration within the network contribute to the skills of teachers in this school?

The literacy lead is bringing in good classroom practice ideas from the network. She is also finding that the network offers her a lot of support in how to approach teachers and get them to try the new practices.

Example

The literacy lead was at a loss for how to enter the teachers' classrooms to observe them without imposing because she wanted to make sure that they were comfortable with her presence and open to her feedback. She used a process developed with the literacy network team where she first approached the teachers already motivated to try the new strategies, and then had them talk about the observation at a staff meeting promoting the idea of useful support within the school.

Joan: In reading through the answers to collaboration, I get the sense that it is not where you want it to be.

Elsie: Not at all. We are really struggling with this. The teachers know and respect each other. The relationships are really great. You saw the evidence. But we just can't get them to that critical phase where they are really working together on their weaknesses and capitalizing on their strengths.

Rochelle: I have been walking on eggshells to get into most classrooms. It has been a hard process because, although the teachers will talk the talk, most are not really opening up. There are four teachers who are willing to open their classrooms. But even then, they will allow their grade colleague in and that is about it. They don't see a strong connection with the others.

Joan: But you have managed to get into all the classrooms now, right?

Rochelle: Yes, I have. It has been a slow process with a little nudging here and there. It has been really useful to have the network for that because I have been able to use the network. I told the teachers that all schools in the network are doing observations and so we need to move forward with it. That has helped—using that external pressure.

Sophie:	The staff is motivated. Please don't misunderstand. It is just that they feel very protective of their classrooms and their kids.
Joan:	And I read that as a challenge. The staff are being protective of the kids in their classrooms and the idea is to get them to realize that these kids are part of a bigger school and that they need to share that responsibility.
Sophie:	I am not disagreeing with you. I am just telling you how our teachers think. And because they think this way, it is really hard to get them to collaborate at a deep level.
Joan:	Is it possible to use the Grade 2 and 4 teachers who are doing it as an example to promote collaboration in the school?
Rochelle:	What do you mean?
Joan:	Well, can we put pressure on the teachers to open their groups . . . maybe extend to the next grade? So that the Grade 2 teachers include the Grade 3 teachers and the Grade 4 teachers include the Grade 5 teachers?
Rochelle:	I suggested it. They say okay and then don't do it.
Elsie:	I have also mentioned it at staff meetings and supported Rochelle as much as possible.
Joan:	Well, asking them to collaborate is very different from giving them a shared task that requires them to work together—a project that involves joint work with a deadline.
Sophie:	Hmmm, if we are looking at inference as a whole-school issue, then we should be able to find cross-grade tasks.
Elsie:	But it can't just be a task. It needs to be something that is useful for them at the end or they will regard it as extra work. I won't consider it successful if they don't come out of it thinking that they could not have done as good a job if they did not work on it together.
Joan:	I agree. It needs to be practical and useful and directly related to their work and the focus.
Rochelle:	I wonder whether we can have it so that the map—the concept map for inference and literacy—should be part of the work.
Elsie:	That would give it the profile that we want. Especially if the map is going to be up on the wall and distributed throughout the school.
Sophie:	That is a good idea. But it needs to be linked to the work that we are doing now and not remain theoretical.
Rochelle:	Let me think about this some more. I want to ask my literacy lead group about it, and develop something based on what worked in their schools. Some of them have already been asking their teachers work together on different projects.

Joan: Okay. When you do that, it is important for you to look at what was written in the reflections about your school: the teachers are not seeing the kids as "our kids." You need work that is going to highlight the effect of the school as a whole . . . something that highlights the continuation from Grades 2 to 5 and how each student is affected by the series of teachers that they have and not the individual teacher.

The group continued to talk through the ideas on promoting sustainable collaboration that was rooted in the work. Joan had some good examples from her own experiences that she shared, and they talked through how some of them would work in this school's context.

FROM COLLABORATIVE INQUIRY TO INSTRUCTIONAL LEADERSHIP ACTIONS

Collaborative analysis of student learning (CASL) can be very powerful because it provides a focused forum for teacher learning (predicated on an evidence-based student learning need) that is driven by inquiry. There is the connection to curriculum, research, and subject expertise through the presence of a "knowledgeable other," and there is built-in accountability. But the accountability mechanism isn't about surveillance or judgment. It is about professional learning grounded in evidence. Many of the learning networks with which we are involved tend to work with six-week cycles between the CASL professional learning sessions for any given teacher. The individual cycles are staggered such that in any given week there is a different set of focused teachers.

At the next meeting of the principals group, members reflected on their joint findings from the critical friend site visits and interviews. Their practical discussions of how to lead the change consisted of uploading ideas from the schools to the network.

After all of the critical friend interviews had been conducted in the schools, the principals had a network meeting to discuss their shared issues and set the "leader learning" priority areas. Each principal agreed to identify three priorities derived from the data for their own school, and share it with the group. When the group went through the list together, it identified two shared issues: (1) effectively managing school time for regular CASL sessions, and (2) managing regular data collection to monitor teaching improvements.

Rita: It sounds like the CASL sessions are really effective in the schools.

Elsie: Absolutely! It has been a key in getting my teachers to genuinely collaborate. They are finding that it is useful in helping their in-class practice.

Rikard: I agree, it is effective. But it is a double-edged sword. On the one hand, my literacy lead is telling me that she is seeing some real instructional changes, and

	on the other hand, my teachers are telling me that they need time allocated to CASL because there are a lot more students that need targeted help.
Rita:	I am there too. I have teachers who want to do more of them, but we don't have the time for it.
Charles:	I did have that issue and then my literacy lead asked me to pilot a new strategy that has actually solved the organizational issue and has benefited the entire school.
Rita:	Is this related to that Reading Buddies pilot you are doing?
Charles:	Yes, that is it.
Rita:	My literacy lead has been talking to me about it, but I really have not had time to think about another strategy in the school.
Elsie:	I have heard about it too, but I don't see what it has to do with CASL.
Charles:	Let me first describe the program so you can see that it is completely related to our focus. The Reading Buddies program involves the intentional pairing of older children with younger ones in structured activities that are supervised by half the teachers while the others have their time released. For example, Grade 2 and Grade 6 students might be paired such that in one week the Grade 2 teachers supervise the reading buddies while the Grade 6 teachers run their CASL sessions and then the following week it switches. We have organized the schedule so that there are two a month, and it includes all the grade levels. The older students are using guides to support the younger students in making inferences from stories. The older students have reported that they are enjoying the activity. Moreover, the teachers of the older students are taking advantage of the program to support the students' learning through training in reading strategies. It is a win–win situation.
Elsie:	That does sound good, but the organizational management must have been a nightmare at the start.
Charles:	Yes, it was a bit sticky, but I can pass on the model to you if you are interested.
Rikard:	That is one strategy that works. I am not sure about Reading Buddies, but I do think that a school-wide program where half the teachers are released from their teaching duties to run CASL is a great idea.

The group of principals continued to exchange ideas on how to be more effective with the school time that they managed. When they exhausted the conversation about time, they moved on to systematic data collection for monitoring improvements. They quickly recognized that this was a very important point and that they needed to learn more about it. They had each been involved in collecting data on behalf of the district for their school improvement plan, but this was different. They needed to really think through the monitoring piece and how they could manage a system that was practical and useful to make evidence-informed decisions. The leadership team identified it as its next leader learning priority.

At this point, the inevitable question we get asked is where schools find the time for this kind of ongoing, job-embedded professional learning. This is precisely why getting the focus right is so important. The lack of focus that characterizes many school-based PLCs that they often become expensive activity traps with significant opportunity costs attached to them. We've made a big deal about the focus—about getting to it and about sticking to it until there is evidence to suggest it is time to move on—because the focus should reflect a sense of priority and urgency that is unequalled when it comes to setting the improvement agenda. As it turns out, schools are right in that a shortage of time is experienced. However, it often isn't a case of finding more time (a good thing, since this isn't an option!); rather, it means being more efficient and intentional with the available time. Educators are often surprised when we share the results of some of the various studies that have been done about "where the time goes." They are surprised to learn, for example, that out of over 1,000 hours per year of mandated time by the state, only about 300 of those hours end up as quality academic learning time. The rest of time goes to things like absences, lunch, recess, transitions, and all of the other "activities" that take up class time (Weinstein & Mignano, 2003). We are not saying that things like recess and lunch are unimportant. But less than one-third of the time that we think we have is actually dedicated to student learning. The remaining time isn't lost in big chunks. Instead, time drifts away in minutes—five minutes here, fifteen minutes there. But these small incremental losses add up. That's why it is important to be intentional and efficient in controlling how time is used.

The most successful networks we know privilege within-school focused professional learning time to the extent that all of the schools in the network actually timetable it in, just as they would with, say, a literacy block. That is, they build opportunities for structured collaborative inquiry, like CASL, right into the school day. They do it by separating professional learning from operational issues at staff meetings; if an operational issue can go in a memo, it does. They do it by using the staffroom for operational conversations and then moving professional learning opportunities into classrooms as reminders of what it is that they are there for. And they do it by using grade team and divisional meetings to move the focus forward.

Time for Reflection

How could you adapt the "critical friend interview" for use in your context?

Brainstorm a list of activities in which you have been engaged that you would call instructional leadership, and give your reasoning for choosing these activities.

Plan some activities (and strategies) to ensure that ideas get uploaded and downloaded between the schools and the network.

8

Sustaining Networked Learning Communities

Networks have the potential to be efficient units of engagement for school districts. The top-down structural relationship between districts and schools makes it challenging for district central offices to engage with schools on an individual basis. Despite the fact that there is good evidence that schools benefit from the kind of external facilitation and relationships that districts can provide (Stringfield, 1998), the simple reality is that central office supports (and pressures) are often thinly stretched across the schools in a system—that is, school-based demand exceeds central office supply. What this means is that district central offices are always looking for efficient ways to engage with schools and, more often than not, this means some kind of volume-based approach, using strategies like the withdrawal model of professional development—for example, where educators came out of their schools and get together *en masse* (in a hotel ballroom or the equivalent) for the purpose of some kind of in-service capacity-building opportunity. The supply/demand imbalance makes the appeal of this kind of a strategy easy to understand, but there is a significant downside that is nicely expressed in the words of one of our workshop participants, who spoke of the challenge of moving the learning "from the ballroom to the classroom." Bridging the gulf between ballroom and classroom is about finding (or rather making) localized meaning. It requires new learning that grows out of, and is anchored in, school-based needs and contextual peculiarities. This is why notions of job-embedded professional learning are lauded: because they are meaningful. Learning is meaning making. And meaning making is personal. Districts need to find ways to support this kind of localized meaning making. Networked learning communities (NLCs)—as an intermediary structure between schools and the district—can help with this. A group of schools organized around a common and needs-based (localized) learning focus makes for a sensible unit that the district can use to target its support.

By now, it has become obvious that creating and supporting NLCs represents a worthwhile but challenging undertaking that takes time and commitment. And it does not have an ending. School improvement is fundamentally a process of continuous adaptation and change. This means that people who work in contemporary schools will always have to be learners themselves in their work. Improving the experience and the outcomes of schooling for all children is like a rotating puzzle. Over and over again, educators need to work with available information and approaches to fashion the best solution.

Sustainability is a double-pronged issue for NLCs. On one hand, NLCs hold the promise of being an organizational form that can help sustain continuous learning and capacity building over an extended period of time. But they are intrinsically fragile and difficult to sustain. In this chapter, we explore sustainability from both of these perspectives.

Fullan (2004) defines sustainability as "the capacity of a system to engage in the complexities of continuous improvement" (p. ix). Hargreaves and Fink (2005) define it as "leadership and improvement [that] preserves and develops deep learning for all that spreads and lasts" (p. 17). For these authors, sustainability means more than whether something lasts. It implies that groups continually learn from their experiences with the change and they continue to develop capacity in what they are attempting to change. This approach to sustainability means that change is part of the individual's and group's way of working—it is a taken-for-granted part of how they think and act, as they continually strive to build capacity to support student learning. Sustainability is not conformity and the dogged pursuit of some mandate. It is grounded in sustaining improvement, not particular actions. The challenge is striking a balance between fidelity and innovation, making the connections among various initiatives and coordinating the activities of various groups to ensure that schools are not inundated with confusing and inconsistent messages, understand how things go together, and establish improvement agendas that both continue over time and are adapted and revised to be more efficient and effective.

NLCs are ideal structures to foster the sustainability of change in schools. They provide the forum for educators to challenge existing practices, consider a range of alternatives, create professional learning opportunities for everyone involved, broaden the base of leadership, weather personnel changes, and build local ownership. Hopkins and Jackson (2002) describe the role networks can play in times of change:

> In the past, most school systems have operated almost exclusively through individual units—be they teachers, departments, schools or local agencies. Such isolation may have been appropriate during times of stability but during times of change there is a need to tighten the loose coupling, to increase collaboration and to establish more fluid and responsive structures.

NLCs are structures that bring people together for focused collaborative inquiry, focused instructional leadership, and focused professional learning, in the service of learning for students.

SUSTAINING COLLECTIVE UNDERSTANDING

Dalin and Rolff (1995) argue that the only way schools will survive the future is to have the capacity to deal with change because they have a collective understanding of where they are going, what is important, and how to get there. Sustainability of positive changes in education depends on attention to collective development. Individual learning is no longer sufficient. People at all levels of the system need to learn and different parts of the system must be aligned to provide a coherent and consistent picture and strategy for change (Stoll, in press).

It is much easier to imagine collective understanding than it is to actually reach it. Education has traditionally been a profession of individuals, working in privacy and isolation from their peers. Collective understanding means moving outside idiosyncratic personal views, establishing a common language, and ensuring that concepts are also understood in the same way. In our experience, it takes considerable time, attention to evidence, and conversation to agree about a common focus, with people often thinking that they agree—until they engage in serious dialogue. Dialogue is a community process in which all participants play an equal role, suspending their individual assumptions as they enter into a genuine "thinking together" (Senge, 1990). In connecting learning communities, dialogic processes are oriented toward articulating and exploring members' tacit knowledge, presuppositions, ideas, and beliefs, bringing them to the surface, examining them, and challenging them in relation to the tacit knowledge of others and the explicit knowledge of theory research and practice. In learning communities, the dialogue takes place as learning conversations—focused conversations with an overt learning goal. A learning conversation is a planned and systematic approach taken to professional dialogue that supports community members to reflect on and improve their practice.

SUSTAINING PROFESSIONAL LEARNING

Building capacity for change is much more than professional development for individual teachers. Stoll (in press) defines capacity as the power to engage in and sustain learning of people at all levels of the educational system for the collective purpose of enhancing student learning. Capacity is a quality that allows people, individually and collectively, to routinely learn from the world around them and to apply this learning to new situations so they can continue on a path toward their goals in an ever-changing context (Stoll & Earl, 2003).

It may ultimately be up to each teacher to take charge of her or his own continuous learning. However, working in learning communities and networks shapes this learning and embeds it in a social and job-embedded context that has the power to allow large groups of teachers to become competent and confident about new teaching content and approaches that may be fundamentally different from past practice. New ways of learning don't come easily; learning means coming to terms with different ideas and ways of doing things. This usually necessitates trying something out again and again, tinkering, working at it, feeling uncomfortable for a while, and experiencing new responses. The danger in many change efforts is that teachers develop considerable enthusiasm as they implement the change, but over time the momentum fades as difficult problems surface and opportunities for continued and intensive learning are not available.

NLCs push educators to take the lead in their own continuous learning—to establish their own goals, create practical images of the learning, get support from peers, learn together, practice in their classrooms, engage in regular feedback and self-evaluation, and persevere when the learning gets tough (Stoll, Fink, & Earl, 2003).

SUSTAINING AND BROADENING LEADERSHIP

All too often, innovation in education founders because of changes in leadership. One of the most significant events in the life of a school that is most likely to bring about a sizeable shift in direction is a change of leadership. Although waves of reform exert the greatest and most immediate pressures on whole systems, it is changes of leaders and leadership that most directly and dramatically provoke change in individual schools (A. Hargreaves & Fink, 2005). Changes in leadership can have an immediate and often dramatic impact on a school's focus and direction, creating uncertainty and affecting the pace of improvement efforts. Frequent changes often mean an anxious and uncertain organizational climate that does not support the risk taking and experimentation necessary for both individual and collective development (Little, 2005).

NLCs can protect against dramatic changes in direction within schools. When schools are part of networks, guided by a high-leverage focus that is rooted in student needs, both formal and informal leaders in schools and the network have been involved in a process of taking charge of change, based on a collective understanding of where they are going and what is important, with many people taking responsibility for the improvement work. This broad base of leadership can support the school through administrative changes because the group is comfortable with engaging in careful investigation, discussion, reflection, planning, and decision making directed at changing the routine practices of the school. When leadership is distributed and many people are involved in the decisions, the improvement plans are much less susceptible to the whims of a new leader. Instead, new leaders have the advantage of moving into an environment where improvement conversations are the norm and the formal leadership role is defined by an existing focus and plan and becomes one of preserving past successes, staying the course, keeping the improvement going, and monitoring the process until there is evidence that their efforts are making a difference.

SUSTAINING POWERFUL NLCs

NLCs that stimulate and nurture change in classrooms across a number of schools may be powerful mechanisms for improvement but they are also fragile and difficult to sustain. Networks can be susceptible to "activity traps" and can be easily derailed, or they can languish as marginal structures with little action or influence. Just forming a network is not enough. Networks require ongoing attention to both the logistics and to the high-level thinking necessary to challenge deeply held beliefs and embed new and more effective ideas and practices into schools.

NLCs are much more than meetings of personnel across schools. They are the venue for bold thinking, for innovation, for serious attention to evidence, for clarifying ideas, for reserving judgment, for learning beyond what is already known, and for turning lofty ideas into concrete changes in professional practice. As we have argued throughout this book, the value of networks will depend on the clarity and the legitimacy of their learning focus for student and teacher learning, the strength of the instructional leadership (both formal and informal), and the willingness of all to engage in collaborative inquiry that challenges thinking and practice, as a routine way of pursuing better learning for students.

At the next principals' meeting, there was a palpable positive energy in the room. The principals recognized how much they had accomplished and were confident that, even though they did not know the next steps for the network, they did trust in the process. They knew that they could evolve and stay focused.

When the principals met again, they were excited about the range of ways that their teachers were finding to continue working together and they were a little nervous about the next stage of monitoring conversations. It was clear that they needed more than periodic critical friend visits to get the information that they needed to provide support for their teachers. Carl had agreed to talk to them about some data-collection possibilities that the district had been considering to see whether they might be useful for the network.

When Carl began, he stopped and looked at Joan for a minute. Then he went on.

"I think I have some news that should come before we talk about the data. I met with Joan yesterday to tell her that the district has decided that she is the right principal to take over at Peterson Secondary. You all know that Mike has been sick and he's told us that he's not going to be back. It's a tough school and it needs strong leadership. So we have asked Joan to move there."

His announcement was greeted with stunned silence.

Charles:	I don't know what to say. Ordinarily it would be congratulations. But all I can think is "What about us?" Of course you'll stay as part of the network, won't you?
Joan:	That's what Carl and I talked about last night. I don't think so. It doesn't make sense. I'm going to a secondary school. The focus will be different, and that's what the network is for—to identify and stay with a focus until we really make a difference. But, hey—I won't stop being a friend, even a critical friend when you want one. And I imagine I'm going to need a lot of help at Peterson. It will be like starting over, with a steep learning curve.
Rita:	I am in shock, I think. How are we going to carry on with this work without you? You are the core. I have learned so much from you.
Carl:	Exactly, you have learned so much—all of you, from Joan and from each other through the incredible work that you have been accomplishing. Now we have to think about what we need to do to keep it all going. Losing Joan does mean change, and we need to talk through how we will work together to keep it all going.
Rikard:	Okay, number 1: if we are losing Joan, we need to plan a proper party to say goodbye to our first exiting member. A party to celebrate what we have done so far! We can even involve teachers and use it as an occasion to consolidate our work and share it. I bet you'd rather have that than a cake and flowers, wouldn't you Joan?
Joan:	Quite right. Let's do it. Can I be on the planning team? It should be a network celebration so I can participate in planning it. It can also be a time to bring my successor at Selkirk on board. I'm sure there will be an announcement soon about who that will be and this would be a great chance for whoever it is to meet all of you and to really get a feel for what we've been doing.

Charles: Hey you guys, before we get overtaken by planning a party, we can't forget that we have to carry on with our leadership learning. Carl, I'm not sure we can concentrate on data today, so can we arrange another meeting to think about a process for looking at the data for monitoring? In fact, maybe a couple of us can work together beforehand and come up with some suggestions. I have a data guy in my mathematics department who loves to think about this stuff and has just started his masters part time. He might have some good suggestions. Yikes, I just realized we also need another co-chair for the network, if Joan is gone.

Carl: Sure, we can book another day. As for a new co-leader, that's up to the network.

Charles: I'm happy to stay on with a new partner if that's okay with everyone else.

Rikard: I'm happy with that and I should be ready to be co-chair next time, but right now, I'm swamped. Elsie or Rita, is either of you ready to take this on?

Rita: I've been thinking since this meeting started. I have been really scared of the work related to the literacy focus because I don't have a strong literacy background. But, having watched Joan lead the group, I think I'd like to try it.

Elsie: That suits me fine. I really learned a lot working on the critical friend interviews and I can pick up particular tasks like that in the future.

Rikard: That works for me too. In fact, this data stuff intrigues me and I look forward to this next step.

They spent the rest of the meeting planning the network celebration to focus on what their schools were doing together and to celebrate their progress, as well as point the direction towards deep, sustained changes that would benefit their kids.

As they neared the end of their discussion, Joan raised her coffee cup in a toast—to learning for all kids, all teachers and all leaders—because we deserve it!

Time for Reflection

What professional learning do you (individually and collectively) need in order to maintain and improve on your school's performance?

How will you use the network to establish and sustain your school's improvement agenda?

What will you contribute to the network to ensure that it remains robust and provides the forum for sustained improvement in network schools?

References

Allen, K., & Cherrey, C. (2000). *Systemic leadership: Enriching the meaning of our work.* Boston: University Press of America.

Barber, M. (2002, April 23). *From good to great: Large-scale reform in England.* Paper presented at Futures of Education conference, Zurich, Switzerland.

Bolam, R., McMahon, A., Stoll, L., Thomas, S., Wallace, M., Greenwood, A., Hawkey, K., Ingram, S., Atkinson, A., & Smith, M. (2005). *Creating and sustaining effective professional learning communities.* . Nottingham, UK: Department for Education and Skills..

Borko, H. (2004). Professional development and teacher learning: Mapping the terrain. *Educational Researcher, 33*(8), 3–15.

Bransford, J., Brown, A., & Cocking. R. (1999). *How people learn: Brain, mind, experience, and school.* Washington, DC: National Academy of Sciences National Research Council.

Bryk, A., Camburn, E., & Louis, K. S. (1999). Professional community in Chicago elementary schools: Facilitating factors and organizational consequences. *Educational Administration Quarterly, 35,* 751–781.

Bryk, A., & Schneider, B. (2002). *Trust in schools: A core resource for improvement.* New York: Russell Sage Foundation.

Center for Research on the Context of Teaching. (2003). *Bay Area School Reform Collaborative Summary Report: Phase I: 1996–2001.* Stanford, CA: Author.

Chapman, J., & Aspin, D. (2003). Networks of learning: A new construct for educational provision and a new strategy for reform. In B. Davies, & J. West-Burnham (Eds.), *Handbook of educational leadership and management* (pp. 653–659). London: Pearson.

Church, M., Bitel, M., Armstrong, K., Fernando, P., Gould, H. Joss, S., et al. (2002). *Participation, relationships and dynamic change: New thinking on evaluating the work of international networks.* London: University College.

Cross, R., & Parker, A. (2004). *The hidden power of social networks: How work really gets done in organizations.* Boston: Harvard Business School.

Dalin, P., & Rolff, H. G. (1995). *Changing the school culture.* London: Cassell.

Darling-Hammond, L., & Richardson, N. (2009). Teacher learning: What matters? *Educational Leadership, 66*(5), 46–53.

DuFour, R., & Eaker, R. (1998). *Professional learning communities at work.* Atlanta: ASCD.

Earl, L., & Katz, S. (2005). *What makes a network a learning network?* Nottingham, UK: National College for School Leadership.

Earl, L., & Katz, S. (2006). *Leading schools in a data-rich world: Harnessing data for school improvement.* Thousand Oaks, CA: Corwin.

Earl, L., & Katz, S. (2007). Leadership in networked learning communities: Defining the terrain. *School Leadership and Management, 27*(3), 239–258.

Earl, L., Katz, S., & Ben Jaafar, S. (2008). *Facilitator's guide for leading in a data-rich world: Harnessing data for school improvement.* Thousand Oaks, CA: Corwin.

Earl, L., Katz, S., Elgie, S., Ben Jaafar, S., & Foster, L. (2006). *How networked learning communities work*, Volume 1: *The report*. Nottingham, UK: National College for School Leadership.

Earl, L., & Timperley, H. (Eds.) (2008). *Professional learning conversations: Challenges in using evidence for improvement*. Milton Keynes, UK: Springer.

Elmore, R. (2002). The limits of "change." *Harvard Education Letter Research Online*. Retrieved April 15, 2009, from http://www.edletter.org/past/issues/2002-jf/limit sofchange.shtml.

Elmore, R. (2007). Professional networks and school improvement. *School Administrator*, *64*(4), 20–24

Engestrom, Y. (1999). From iron cages to webs on wind: Three theses on themes and learing at work. *Lifelong Learning in Europe*, *4*(2), 101–110.

Firestone, W., & Pennell, J. (1997). State-initiated teacher networks: A comparison of two cases. *American Educational Research Journal*, *34*(2), 237–268.

Fullan, M. (2004). *Leadership and sustainability*. Thousand Oaks, CA: Sage.

Glaser, R., & Chi, M. (1988). Introduction: What is it to be an expert? In M. Chi, R. Glaser, & M. Farr (Eds.), *The nature of expertise* (pp. xv–xxvii). Hillsdale, NJ: Lawrence Erlbaum.

Hakkarainen, K., Palonen, T., Paavola, S., & Lehtinen, E. (2004). *Communites of networked expertise: Professional and educational perspectives*. Amsterdam: Elsevier.

Halverson, R. (2003). Systems of practice: How leaders use artifacts to create professional community in schools. *Educational Policy Analysis Archives*, *11*(37). Retrieved April 15, 2009, from http://epaa.asu.edu/epaa/v11n37.

Hargreaves, A. (1994). *Changing teachers, changing times: Teachers' work and culture in the postmodern age*. London: Cassell.

Hargreaves, A., & Fink, D. (2005). *Sustainable leadership*. New York: John Wiley and Sons.

Hargreaves, D. (2003). *Working laterally: How innovative networks make an education epidemic*. London: Demos/NCSL.

Harris, A. (2001). Building the capacity for school improvement. *School Leadership and Management*, *21*(30), 261–270.

Heller, M., & Firestone, W. (1995). Who's in charge here? Sources of leadership for change in eight schools. *Elementary School Journal*, *96*(1), 65–86.

Herman, J., & Gibbons, B. (2001). *Lessons learned in using data to support school inquiry and continuous improvement*. Final Report to the Stuart Foundation. Los Angeles, CA: Center for the Study of Evaluation, UCLA.

Holcomb. E. (1999). *Getting excited about data: How to combine people, passion, and proof*. Thousand Oaks, CA: Corwin.

Hopkins, D., & Jackson, D. (2002). *Building capacity for leading and learning*. Nottingham, UK: National College of School Leadership.

Hudson-Ross, S. (2001). Intertwining opportunities: Participants' perceptions of professional growth within multiple-site teachers education network at the secondary level. *Teaching and Teacher Education*, *17*(4), 433–54.

Jackson, D., & Temperley, J. (2006, January). *From professional learning community to networked learning community*. Paper presented at the International Conference on School Effectiveness and Improvement, Fort Lauderdale, FL.

Katz, S. (2007). *Scaling up from one network to many: The establishment of networked learning communities within the district*. Markham, ON: York Region District School Board.

Katz, S., & Earl, L. (2005). *Research report: Classroom assessment*. Toronto, ON: Greater Toronto Area Professional Network Centre.

Katz, S., & Earl, L. (2006). Redefining educational accountability: Towards informed professional judgment. *Changing Perspectives*, *1*(3), 2–6.

Katz, S., Earl, L., Ben Jaafar, S., Elgie, S., Foster, L., Halbert, J., & Kaser, L. (2008). Learning networks: They key enablers of successful knowledge communities. *McGill Journal of Education*, *43*(2), 111–138.

Katz, S., Earl, L., & Dack, L. A. (2008). *Networking to build local capacity*. Toronto, ON: Greater Toronto Area Professional Network Centre.

Katzenmeyer, M., & Moller, G. (2001). *Awakening the sleeping giant: Helping teachers develop as leaders* (2nd ed.). Thousand Oaks, CA: Corwin.

Langer, G., Colton, A., & Goff, L. (2003). *Collaborative analysis of student work: Improving teaching and learning*. Alexandria, VA: ASCD.

Leithwood, K., Mascall, B., Strauss, T., Sacks, R., Memon, N., & Yashkina, A. (2007). Distributing leadership to make schools smarter: Taking the ego out of the system. *Leadership and Policy in Schools, 6*, 37–67.

Lieberman, A., & Grolnick, M. (1996). Networks and reform in American education. *Teachers College Record, 98*(1), 7–45.

Lieberman, A., & Wood, D. (2002). *Inside the National Writing Project: Connecting network learning and classroom teaching*. New York: Teachers College Press.

Little, J. W. (1990). The persistence of privacy: Autonomy and initiative in teachers' professional relations. *Teachers College Record, 91*(4), 509–536.

Little, J. W. (2005). *Nodes and nets: Investigating resources for professional learning in schools and networks*. Unpublished paper for National College for School Leadership, Nottingham, UK.

MacBeath, J. (1988). "I didn't know he was ill": The role and value of the critical friend, in L. Stoll & K. Myers (Eds.), *No quick fixes: Perspectives on school in difficulty* (pp. 118–132). London: Falmer Press.

Marzano, R., Pickering, D., & Pollock, J. (2001). *Classroom instruction that works: Research-based strategies for increasing student achievement*. Alexandria, VA: Association for Supervision and Curriculum Development.

McLaughlin, M., & Talbert, J. (2001). *Professional communities and the work of high school teaching*. Chicago: University of Chicago Press.

Mitchell, C., & Sackney, L. (2001). Building capacity for a learning community. *Canadian Journal of Educational Administration and Policy, 19*. Accessed February 14, 2004, from www.umanitoba.ca/publications/cjeap/issues19.html.

Newell, S., & Swan, J. (2000). Trust and inter-organizational networking. *Human Relations, 53*(10), 1287–1328.

Nonaka, I., & Takeuchi, H. (1995). *The knowledge-creating company*. Oxford, UK: Oxford University Press.

OECD (1997). *Sustainable flexibility: A prospective study on work, family and society in the information age*. Paris: OECD.

Passer, M., Smith, R., Atkinson, M., Mitchell, J., & Muir, D. (2005). *Psychology frontiers & applications* (2nd Canadian ed.). Toronto: McGraw-Hill Ryerson.

Piaget, J. (1967). *Six psychological studies*. London: University Press.

Robinson, V. (2007). *School leadership and student outcomes: Identifying what works and why?* William Walker Oration, Australian Council for Educational Leaders (ACEL), Sydney, Australia..

Rowan, B. (1990). Commitment and control: Alternative strategies for the organizational design of schools. *Review of Research in Education, 16*, 353–392.

Schmoker, M. (2004). Start here for improving teaching. *The School Administrator, 61*(10), 48.

Senge, P. (1990). *The fifth discipline: The art and practice of the learning organization*. New York: Doubleday.

Sherrill, J. (1999). Preparing teachers for leadership roles in the 21st century. *Theory Into Practice, 38*, 56–59.

Smith, A., & Wohlstetter, P. (2001). Reform through school networks: A new kind of authority and accountability. *Educational Policy, 15*(4), 499–519.

Spillane, J. (2006). *Distributed leadership*. San Francisco: Jossey-Bass.

Spillane, J., Camburn, E., & Pareja, A. (2007). Taking a distributed perspective to the school principal's workday. *Leadership and Policy in Schools, 6*, 103–125.

Stein, M. K., & Nelson, B. (2003). Leadership content knowledge. *Educational Evaluation and Policy Analysis, 25*(4), 423–448.

Stoll, L. (in press). Connecting learning communities: Capacity building for systemic change. In A. Hargreaves, A. Lieberman, M. Fullan, & D. Hopkins (Eds.), *Second international handbook of educational change*. Dordrecht: Springer.

Stoll, L., & Earl, L. (2003). Making it last: Building capacity for sustainability. In B. Davies & J. West-Burnham (Eds.), *The handbook of educational leadership and management* (pp. 491–504). London: Pearson Education.

Stoll, L., & Fink, D. (1996). *Changing our schools: Linking school effectiveness and school improvement*. Buckingham, UK: Open University Press.

Stoll, L., Fink, D., & Earl, L. (2003). *It's about learning and it's about time*. London: Falmer Press.

Stringfield, S. (1998). Organizational learning and current reform efforts. In K. Leithwood & K. S. Louis (Eds.), *Schools as learning communities* (pp. 255–268). Lisse, The Netherlands: Swets & Zeitlinger.

Supovitz, J. (2006). *The case for district-based reform: Leading, building, and sustaining school improvement*. Cambridge, MA: Harvard University Press.

Supovitz, J., & Christman, J. (2005). Small learning communities that actually learn: Lessons for school leaders. *Phi Delta Kappan, 86*, 649–651.

Surowiecki, J. (2004). *The wisdom of crowds: Why the many are smarter than the few*. London: Abacus.

Timperley, H. (2004). *Situating networked learning communities in international research coherence and networked learning communities: A distributed leadership perspective*. Paper commissioned by Aporia Consulting, Toronto, ON.

Timperley, H., & Robinson, V. (2003). Workload and the professional culture of teachers. In L. Kydd, L. Anderson, & W. Newton (Eds.), *Leading people and teams in education* (pp. 151–168). London: Sage.

Timperley, H., Wilson, A., Barrar, H., & Fung, I. (2008). *Teacher professional learning and development: Best evidence synthesis iteration (BES)*. Wellington, New Zealand: Ministry of Education.

Von Krogh, G., Ichijo, K., & Nonaka, I. (2000). *Enabling knowledge creation*. New York: Oxford University Press.

Weinstein, C., & Mignano, A. (2003). *Elementary classroom management*. New York: McGraw Hill.

West-Burnham, J., & Otero, G. (2004). *Educational leadership and social capital*. Incorporated Association of Registered Teachers of Victoria Seminar Series, August, no. 136.

Wohlstetter, P., & Smith, A. (2000, March). A different approach to systemic reform: Network structures in Los Angeles. *Phi Delta Kappan, 81*, 508–515.

York-Barr, J., & Duke, K. (2004). What do we know about teacher leadership? Findings from two decades of scholarship. *Review of Educational Research, 74*(3), 255–316.